Walk a New Path

Forgiveness, Grieving and the Twelve Steps

Sylvain Lavoie, OMI

Foreword by Richard Rohr, OFM

© 2015 Novalis Publishing Inc.

Cover design and layout: Audrey Wells
Cover photo: iStockphoto

Published by Novalis

Publishing Office
1 Eglinton Avenue East
Toronto, Ontario, Canada
M4P 3A1

Head Office
4475 Frontenac Street
Montréal, Québec, Canada
H2H 2S2

www.novalis.ca

Lavoie, Sylvain, 1947-, author   Walk a new path : forgiveness, grieving and the twelve steps /
Archbishop Sylvain Lavoie, O.M.I.

ISBN 978-2-89688-184-0 (pbk.)

    1. Forgiveness--Religious aspects--Catholic Church. 2. Grief-- Religious aspects--Catholic Church. I. Title.

BV4647.F55L39 2015   241'.4   C2015-902385-8

Printed in Canada.

All rights reserved. No part of this publication may be reproduced, stored in a retrieval system, or transmitted in any form, or by any means, electronic, mechanical, photocopying, recording, or otherwise, without the written permission of the publisher.

We acknowledge the financial support of the Government of Canada through the Canada Book Fund for business development activities.

5   4   3   21   20   19

Contents

Acknowledgements 7
Foreword by Richard Rohr, O.F.M. 11
Preface 13
The Complete Serenity Prayer 15
A Case Study: Part One 16

Part One: Human Be-ing 20
Some Supportive Voices 20
The Medicine Wheel 21
The Lake of Our Humanity 22
The Role of Thinking or Rational Intelligence 24
The Importance of Emotions 24
Our Basic Human Needs 35
Human Needs and the Great Commandment 38
Met Needs 39
The Awareness Wheel 40
The Wellness Wheel of Met Needs 41
Suggested Activities and Questions for Reflection 44

Part Two: A Spirituality of Recovery and Wellness 45
An Integrated Spirituality 45
Definitions of Spirituality 45
Teepee Spirituality 48
1. The Pole of Faith 49
2. The Pole of Fellowship 49
3. The Pole of Self-awareness 54
Teepee Spirituality, Human Needs and the Great Commandment 56
A Spirituality of Human Incompleteness 59
Suggested Activity and Questions for Reflection 67

Part Three: The Journey into Addiction	68
The Dysfunctional Wheel of Unmet Needs	68
The Unwritten Rules	70
The Survival Roles	71
The Three Options	76
The Three Temptations	77
The Journey into Addiction	80
– The Love Pattern	81
– The Lack of Love Pattern	83
Some Definitions of Addiction	88
A Working Definition of Addiction	91
Kinds of Addictions	93
The Spiritual Cage	96
Our Spiritual Burden	98
Suggested Activities and Question for Reflection	101

Part Four: The Twelve Step Healing Journey	102
The Twelve Steps of Alcoholics Anonymous Adapted	102
The Twelve Step Healing Journey	104
A. Getting into the Program (Steps 1–3)	107
Step One: *Humility and Powerlessness*	107
Step Two: *Faith*	110
Step Three: *Surrender*	113
– The God of Our Understanding	117
– A Compassionate Higher Power	120
B. The Heart of the Program (Steps 4–9)	123
Step Four: *Honesty*	123
Step Five: *Trust*	128
– A Grid for Receiving a Step Five	132
Step Six: *Forgiveness*	133
– The Fourth Way of Forgiveness	134
– Step Six Guide: Forgiveness and Healing	139
Step Seven: *Healing*	151
Step Eight: *Courage*	154
Step Nine: *Reconciliation*	156

C. Living with the Program 161
Step Ten: *Awareness*.. 161
Step Eleven: *Prayer* 164
– Lectio Divina 170
– Prayer of the Anawim 173
Step Twelve: *Sharing and Service*... 175
Suggested Activities 178

**Part Five: Understanding and Integrating
The Twelve Steps**.. 179
The Recovery Wheel 179
Integrating the Twelve Steps 181
The Twelve Steps applied to Teepee Spirituality 182
The Recovery Burger 184
Our Spiritual Burden and the Twelve Steps 186
The Healing Hamburger 187
A Spirituality of Weeding 189
Healing as an Exodus Journey and
Paschal Mystery Experience 192
Stepping through the Exodus Journey and
Paschal Mystery Experience 196
The Spiritual Spiral 198
Suggested Activities 200

A Case Study: Part Two 201
Conclusion 204
Bibliography and Suggested Readings....................................... 205
List of Illustrations 209

Appendices.. 211
1. The Twelve Steps of Alcoholics Anonymous and Disclaimer 211
2. Concerned Intervention 213
3. The Sacrament of Reconciliation and the Twelve Steps 215
4. Twelve by Twenty-Four 218
5. The Twelve Step Beatitudes 220
6. Other Resources 221

Endnotes.. 222

Acknowledgements

Life is a mystery to be lived, not a problem to be solved.

There is much wisdom in this statement. I think I am at a stage in my life where I am closer to living this way.

As a young adult, I must admit I often felt like life was more of a problem to be solved than a mystery to be lived. Without understanding it at the time, I came from a background of workaholism and codependency within our family that had created a very subtle need for healing within me. The good news, however, is that our loving Higher Power accepts us as we are and knows who we can become. So it was for me – my attempts to figure out life led to all kinds of discoveries about God, myself, others and life itself.

I realize that this was made possible by the many people who accepted me as I was and who believed in who I could become. Many were actively working the Twelve Step program of Alcoholics Anonymous (A.A.). It is from people such as these that much of the material in this book originated. To them, and to our God as we understand God, I am deeply grateful.

I would like to express gratitude particularly to some who played a large part in my own personal development. First of all is Archbishop emeritus Adam Exner, O.M.I., whose spiritual direction started my healing journey when I was a young scholastic in 1970. Others are Elizabeth B., who provided support, encouragement and wise counsel in my early days of lecturing on spirituality at the Northwest Alcohol and Drug Abuse Centre in Île-à-la-Crosse, Saskatchewan; the late Alec C., who encouraged me to join the A.A. program in Beauval,

Saskatchewan, even though I was not an alcoholic; and both Ron Rolheiser, O.M.I., and Richard Rohr, O.F.M., who have provided key insights and inspiration. I also want to thank Richard Rohr for his wisdom and knowledge in the foreword he generously wrote for this book.

I am especially grateful to my predecessor, Archbishop emeritus Peter Sutton, O.M.I., for his sensitivity to the hurting Church and for his unflinching support for a healing style of ministry throughout my years as director of the Keewatin Renewal Team in the Archdiocese of Keewatin-The Pas. I also owe a big thank you to Ed and Angie Mihalicz, the other members of that team, for their constant support, ongoing collaboration over the years, and generous sharing of their many gifts.

The comments and questions posed by the clients and staff of Hopeview Halfway House in North Battleford, Saskatchewan, from 1992 to 1998, mistahi maskwa Centre in mâkwa sâkahikan (Loon Lake) First Nation, Treaty # 6 Territory, Saskatchewan, from 2000 to 2005, and other rehabilitation centres where I gave sessions over the years both challenged me and taught me a lot. Other privileged moments of both giving and learning were the many Spiritual Days at Queen's House Retreat and Renewal Centre in Saskatoon, recovery retreats at St. Michael's Retreat House in Lumsden, Saskatchewan, and at Providence Centre in Edmonton, as well as sessions at the Domano Renewal Centre in Prince George, British Columbia.

More recent events were a workshop-retreat for Oblates and lay associates at Star of the North Retreat Centre in St. Albert, Alberta, in 2008, and a keynote presentation at the Catholic Health Association of Saskatchewan convention in Prince Albert in 2009.

I also owe a debt of gratitude to my Oblate religious community for their support and understanding of my at times unconventional way of doing ministry. In a special way, I want to thank Fr. Bill Stang, O.M.I., and Bro. Harley Mapes, O.M.I., for their trust in me and for inviting me to offer sessions on addictions awareness, human development and leadership to the pre-novices at the Oblate pre-novitiate in

Meru, Kenya, in 2003. The same would apply to Fr. Alfred Groleau, O.M.I., who invited me to Pakistan for the same purpose, although that never materialized due to my being named bishop at that time. Former Oblates Claude Sheehy and Kurt Stang also provided priceless Oblate community and intimate friendship that helped shape this material, as did Bro. Thomas Novak, O.M.I., during those early "first fervour" days in Beauval, Saskatchewan.

I want to also thank the two Adrian Dominican women religious, Mary Kastens and Mary Assenmacher, who, along with Fr. Bill Stang, O.M.I., and Fr. Paul Bringleson, made up the archdiocesan residence community within which I lived during the writing of much of this book. Sr. Ethel Detz, O.P., and Sr. Iva Gregory, O.P., were also part of that community for some time, as was Sr. Anne Lewans, O.S.U. I am also indebted to Sr. Kastens, Fr. Joe Jacek, O.M.I., and my good friend the late Rod Donlevy for generously offering to proofread the manuscript. Dustin Booher, Sr. Kastens' nephew, provided expert and invaluable help with the references. The staff and program at Southdown Institute in Ontario provided liminal space for these ideas to grow and mature. I express my thanks and gratitude to all the members of Alcoholics Anonymous, Adult Children of Alcoholics, Al-Anon and Co-dependents Anonymous groups in which I participated over the years.

Support has also come from our archdiocesan personnel, staff and leadership team, all of whom have put up with my periods of absence from the archdiocese while I gave the workshops and retreats that were instrumental in the development of this book.

Sr. Teresita Kambeitz, O.S.U., my spiritual director for over seven years, has also indirectly guided this work in her humble, wise way. Sr. Judy Scheffler, S.S.N.D., a close friend since 1991, provided valuable suggestions that shaped the reflection questions and activities for each chapter. Oblate brothers Louis Andreas and Rusty Gardiner generously shared their expertise in assisting with the graphics in the book.

Of course, this book would not have come to fruition without the help of Joseph Sinasac, publishing director of Novalis, which published my other books, *Drumming from Within* and *Together We Heal*; he was a patient collaborator on this one.

Finally, I am grateful to Bill W., Dr. Bob and the early pioneers of Alcoholics Anonymous, who were inspired to create this powerful Twelve Step healing program, and all those who have helped to sustain the movement for over half a century.

The gratitude I feel is added to that of untold thousands whose lives have been touched and healed by this simple, effective and challenging Twelve Step program.

Foreword

I have been convinced for many years that the spirituality of the Twelve Steps is almost perfectly parallel and complementary to the transformative teaching of Jesus and Paul in the Christian Scriptures. I tried to make that point very specifically in a book I wrote called *Breathing Under Water*. In the years since it was published, I have not received a single questioning of or disagreement with that statement.

In fact, it is amazing to me that more ministers of the Gospel do not see this and make use of the practicality and effectiveness of the Twelve Step program for our many addictions. You cannot avoid its truth by any pious or abstract words, as we too often have with the Gospel itself. Addiction might just be a very good way to understand what the Bible really means by sin, but the program avoids the language of blame and punishment, which has discouraged so many who are already discouraged far too much.

In this time when so many are reacting against formal religion, or have even been hurt by organized religion, it is all the more important that the universal healing message of Jesus is not hampered or lessened because of our mistakes and limitations. It is now crucially important that we find new words, images, practices and metaphors for the healing love of God that is always available, and always has been since "the Spirit first hovered over the chaos" (Genesis 1:2) of first creation.

I think Archbishop Lavoie has found a very creative, readable and believable way to do just that! I am especially impressed that he has seen the importance of "grief work" in very often opening the heart and soul in ways that mere verbal teaching cannot do. Grief is the one emotion that "undoes" us from within and then has the potential to also rebuild us from within. Most other failures we can blame someone for, or blame ourselves for, but with true grief we have to just sit there, like Job on his dung heap (Job 2:8), and there slowly learn the hard lessons of love, forgiveness, patience and compassion. Yet we do not really *learn* these lessons, however; it is *done unto us* almost in spite of ourselves, by osmosis, as grace slowly invades our body, our heart and our consciousness. It is only afterwards that we can say with Job, "I knew you before only by hearsay, but now I see you with my own eyes" (Job 42:5).

Jesus made it very clear in such stories as the Prodigal Son (Luke 15:11f) and the Publican and the Pharisee (Luke 18:9-14) that he believed *we come to God much more by doing it wrong than by doing it right*, but that message was just too hard for the ego to absorb. Paul said it even more directly: "When I am weak, I am strong" (2 Corinthians 12:10). It seems that grace is always a humiliation and a defeat for the ego. So we quickly and unfortunately made church work back into a matter of climbing, attaining, proving and verbal believing, despite Jesus' clear message about a way that Paul eventually described as "the folly of the cross" (1 Corinthians 1:20-25).

The Gospel is a path of descent much more than an ascent. It is a *doing* more than a *thinking*, a surrendering more than an achieving, a healing more than an evacuation plan for the next world. How clever of God to make it this way, so that only the humble and honest – and real – could find him! It is never about worthiness. Who of us are worthy, anyway? The soul knows that it is all God's doing from the beginning.

You have a good teacher here on this path, and he writes about it so well that I can only assume he has taken a path of descent himself. Those are the only teachers you can trust!

Fr. Richard Rohr, O.F.M.
Center for Action and Contemplation
Albuquerque, New Mexico, USA

Preface

In 1978, during the formative days of Alcoholics Anonymous (A.A.) in northern Saskatchewan, a group of us took a risk and organized a Serenity Retreat. Open to all, it took place in the school gym in Île-à-la-Crosse. About 35 people from that community and surrounding area attended.

The retreat master was Ron H. from Lloydminster, Alberta. Sr. Olive MacInnis, S.M.S., Ron's niece and a nurse in the local hospital, had recommended him to us. Ron was a buoyant, gregarious man who delighted in sharing his recovery with others. He generously came to lead this retreat, knowing that only his expenses would be covered.

I will never forget one incident during that retreat as I listened to Ron. Sitting beside me was a young man, just out of jail and obviously suffering from the effects of addiction in his life. As Ron shared his story and wisdom with us, Big Book in one hand, Bible in the other, this young man turned to me with a strange look in his eyes and a catch in his voice, and said, "How come this guy knows so much about me?"

It struck me immediately, with a surge of excitement, exactly what that look in his eyes was. It was hope. I could almost see his mind working, processing, thinking the following thoughts: "This man's past resembles my present, yet look at him now: 12 years sober, a successful businessman, giving a retreat to his fellow alcoholics and obviously delighting in it. Could it be possible that his present, if I follow this Twelve Step path, might be my future? Could I be like him someday?" I was seeing hope being born in one still suffering.

To be a source of hope is the underlying purpose for writing this book. It is intended for persons wanting to recover from any addiction, both chemical and process, wanting to heal from emotional pain and move on towards an addictions-free lifestyle. As such, it is more a pastoral approach to addiction and recovery than an academic or scientific work, as the latter resources are readily available.

This book can also be helpful for anyone wanting to learn more about the Twelve Step program, including those journeying with friends or relatives who are struggling with addiction in their lives. It can serve as an introduction to the Twelve Steps, as a companion on a walk through the steps, and as a guide to working the steps on a daily basis.

It is my hope that the ideas, stories and images in this book, developed over 40 years of dealing with my own issues, as well as journeying with the addicted and their friends and families, will be instrumental in instilling hope within the eyes and hearts of the readers.

If even one person's eyes light up with hope, a hope that will make a difference in that person's life and will help him or her achieve sobriety, joyous and free, and walk a new path, the efforts expended in penning this book will be rewarded.

+ Sylvain Lavoie, O.M.I.
St. Albert, Alberta, Canada

The Complete Serenity Prayer

God, give us grace to accept with serenity
the things that cannot be changed,
courage to change the things
which should be changed,
and the wisdom to distinguish
the one from the other.
Living one day at a time,
enjoying one moment at a time,
accepting hardship as a pathway to peace,
taking, as Jesus did,
this sinful world as it is,
not as I would have it,
trusting that You will make all things right,
if I surrender to Your will,
so that I may be reasonably happy in this life,
and supremely happy with You forever in the next.
Amen.

—Reinhold Niebuhr (1892–1971)

A Case Study: Part One

"Twelve Steps to Reconciliation"

Has anger ever kept you from going to a funeral? The Twelve Steps of Alcoholics Anonymous (A.A.) can help you forgive and experience reconciliation.

That was my experience after three years in my first mission as a young Oblate priest in Beauval. Involvement with the local A.A. group and the Twelve Step program helped me realize a breakthrough in my relationship with my father.

I grew up in what seemed to be a normal French Canadian farming family of eight. The fact that our father was a workaholic, however, had a profound impact on me. I thought I had to earn my father's love.

As I grew older, I became aware that our family lacked the closeness and affection that I saw in other families. Uncomfortable feelings of envy and anger started to emerge within me. Unable to deal with those emotions at that time, I simply repressed and buried them as deeply as I could. By the age of 16, however, I could not repress them anymore. I became a very angry, self-righteous young man who left home convinced that his father had raised him the wrong way and determined to straighten his father out. My righteous anger became a cause. I started writing angry letters to my father, complaining about how he had failed in raising us and chastising him about how wrong he was.

For the next 15 years, I would either stay away from home and write angry letters, or argue with and try to change my father every time I visited. I remember a few times when my attitude and behaviour stole some of the "spirit" from our family Christmas gatherings. One brother-in-law told me years later that he would sometimes leave when I came home, knowing that the inevitable tension would build up and explode into a heated discussion or even an argument between my father and me.

My ordination in 1974 as an Oblate priest only added fuel to the fire. Now I had even more reason to believe that I was right and my father wrong, because I had studied theology. At one point, aware that my father was aging and battling illness, I was so resentful and angry that I wondered if I would even be able to attend his funeral when that time came, let alone preside at the event.

In 1976, I attended a priests' retreat, during which we were encouraged to forgive our parents, especially our fathers. I agreed, said a little prayer and thought it was done. However, the arguing continued, though perhaps a little less heatedly, and nothing really changed in my relationship with him.

Two years later, when I was visiting a family at the La Plonge Indian Residential School grounds near Beauval, I witnessed their six-year-old child asleep, stretched out on her father who was sitting on the couch. As I drove away, it was as if I had taken a mental picture of that scene. I was aware of strong feelings of envy, jealousy, loneliness, anger, resentment, self-pity and blame. The question in my mind was "Why wasn't it like that when I was growing up?"

Slowly there surfaced within me the sickening realization that I had not forgiven my father – indeed, that I *could not*. Those painful emotions, especially anger, were still present to me. I felt fear strike deep within me. Should I quit the priesthood? How could I preach love and forgiveness every Sunday if I could not forgive my own father?

Then, suddenly, the word *powerless* from the Twelve Step program came to mind. The inspiration to work the steps with regard to this dilemma was clear and strong. Without a moment's hesitation I began that process, even as I drove down the hill back to the community.

Step One: I was powerless over my resentment and could not forgive my own father.

Step Two: I believed that God could restore me to sanity.

Step Three: I made a decision to change, to turn this situation over to God.

Step Four: I started making a searching and fearless moral inventory as I crossed the bridge over the Beaver River. This step brought me up short. Instead of the usual focus on my father's behaviour for over 15 years, something like an inner invisible spiritual mirror popped up in which I could see myself clearly and truthfully. For the first time in my life, I realized how much I had done to hurt my father by reacting to his behaviour and acting out of anger towards him instead of forgiving him.

Step Five: I phoned a brother priest as soon as I arrived back at the rectory and shared the whole story with him.

Then *Steps Six* and *Seven:* "Get ready to have God remove this defect of character" and "Humbly ask God to remove all my shortcomings." I was ready. I knew without a doubt that my great defect of character was un-forgiveness towards my father. I shared my situation with the Grey Nuns next door, and with the group at the A.A. meeting that Thursday evening. I also prayed from the heart, and asked God to remove *my* defect of character, *my* inability to forgive my own father, *my* awful, enduring resentment towards him.

The next morning at breakfast, something very interesting happened. I caught myself criticizing Sister Simard's cooking. She was the pastoral worker in the mission, and prepared the meals for our little community of three. By my criticism of her efforts, I realized that I was acting just like my father, who tended to be very critical of my mother. With a shock, I realized that I had become just like my father.

Then the breakthrough happened. Perhaps because of the Marriage Encounter weekend I had taken recently and the help it had given me in dealing with feelings, I was able to make a quantum leap and get inside my father's emotions. It dawned on me that if I was *acting* like my father, perhaps he was *feeling* like me.

Suddenly, for the first time in my life, I knew and understood my father. He was a 78-year-old man, and like me, he was full of bottled-up, painful emotions. However, he never had the opportunity to learn how to deal with those emotions, so they were dealing with him, as mine had been dealing with me. This understanding was God's forgiveness. The anger and resentment simply vanished. The experience was transformational. It had taken me 15 years to arrive at this point, but once I arrived, the forgiveness was instantaneous.

Next came *Steps Eight* and *Nine*: making amends. I drove home after the liturgy that Sunday, sat down at the kitchen table with my father, shared my new understanding with him and asked him to forgive me. I even told him in French that I loved him – *Papa, je t'aime* – the first and only time in my life I ever did that.

The amazing thing is that he changed overnight. I believe he dropped his defences because of the change in me; he forgave me and we were reconciled. We enjoyed two good years together, visiting and talking without arguing, before he died in 1980. I was able to truly celebrate his funeral, because I knew that we had forgiven each other and had been reconciled. What an invaluable gift that was for both of us.

I am forever grateful to this Twelve Step program that guided me into reconciliation with my father. So you see, anyone can use this program to experience forgiveness, healing and reconciliation in their lives.

For years, I thought that this reconciliation was as good as it gets, and continued to live the steps with a sense of gratitude. Then, 11 years after my father died, I participated in an Oblate renewal program in San Antonio, Texas, where a spiritual director and a counsellor teamed up to take this experience to a whole new level. That episode is Part Two of this Case Study, and builds on the contents of the whole book, so it is placed at the end as an afterword, and serves as a footnote to this whole approach to healing through the Twelve Step program.

PART ONE: Human Be-ing

Some Supportive Voices

The fact that this book begins on the premise of what it means to be human is very deliberate. There are many who have influenced me in this conviction and direction. One of the first would have to be the second-century bishop St. Irenaeus, who is reported to have exclaimed, "The glory of God is the human being fully alive." In some ways, that one sentence says it all: the best way to give glory to God is to live life the way our Higher Power created us to live it, as persons who have learned the consummate art of being fully human.

Richard Rohr, O.F.M., founder of the Center for Action and Contemplation in Albuquerque, New Mexico, also encouraged me to be fully human. He once gave a retreat to our Oblate Province. I will never forget his opening comment: "You are who you are who you are – what are you afraid of?" That opening shocked me into greater awareness and growth. At that time of my life, I was afraid that if people really got to know me, they wouldn't like me. My sister-in-law had shared with me her perception that I was afraid to love and to be loved, and deep down, I knew she was right. Although yearning for intimacy, I had to face the painful reality that I might be afraid of it, and had to learn to deal with that truth surfaced by Rohr's comment.

Another particular influence on my thinking in this regard is a comment by St. Eugene de Mazenod, O.M.I., founder of the Missionary Oblates of Mary Immaculate. The advice he gave to the Oblates was to help people be fully human, then to become Christians, and finally to help them become saints.

Ray Dlugos, former director of Southdown, a renewal centre in Ontario for men and women in ministry, shared with participants at a conference a key insight into being human, claiming that there are only two kinds of sin: the attempt to be more than human, or the attempt to be less than human.

To attempt to be more than human is to try to rise above human pain, to suppress our emotions, to deny our weaknesses and to hide behind a façade of false pride. It is a denial of our vulnerability, powerlessness and dependency. To try to be less than human is to act only according to instincts. It is to let ourselves drift into dissipation, to medicate our pain with alcohol or drugs, to give up trying. To illustrate this insight, Dlugos referred to the temptations of Jesus, which we will see in Part Three.

And so it has been over the years: every workshop or session that I have given on the subject of addictions awareness has begun with our call to be first and foremost fully human as the foundation for recovery from addiction. So, what does it mean to live a fully human life? We turn our attention to that question now.

The Medicine Wheel

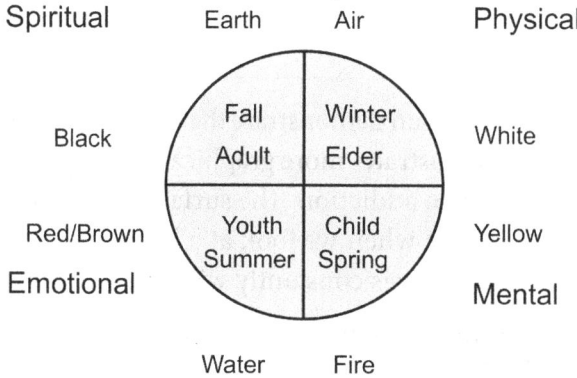

Illustration 01

Most of my ministry over the years has been with the First Nations and Métis. One age-old source of wisdom for them is the Medicine

Wheel. It is also a respected method of effectively passing on the wisdom of the elders. The most basic and familiar teaching of the Medicine Wheel is that to be human is to maintain a harmonious balance of the physical, mental, emotional and spiritual attributes of our makeup as human beings.

In this book, we will be using variations of the Medicine Wheel to explore our common humanity, the reality of addictions in our lives and the journey to recovery and wellness.

The Lake of Our Humanity

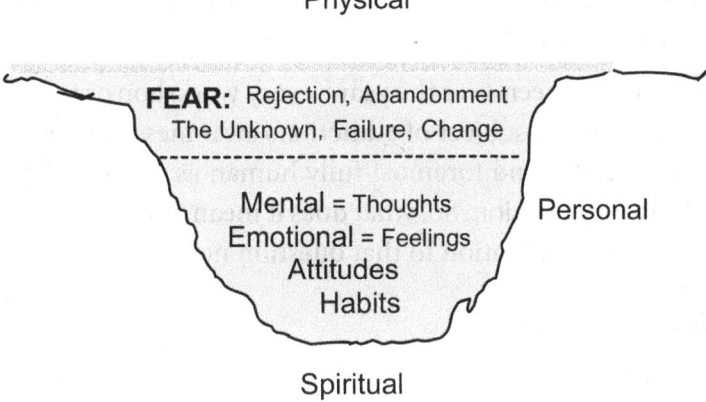

Illustration 02

The image of a lake can demonstrate the teachings of the Medicine Wheel in a way that illustrates more graphically the dynamics of what underlies a tendency to addiction. The surface of the lake represents the *physical*. All we see when we look at a lake is the surface of the water. That surface changes constantly with the touch of the wind.

It is the same interpersonally. What we see when we first meet others is the *physical*. Their appearance and demeanor can change each day. To really know them, we must go deeper, into the *personal*, and get to know their *thoughts* and *emotions*, as symbolized by the water. Even here, emotions are more personal than thoughts. I may have received a particular thought or idea intellectually from someone else or from a book, but my emotions are *my* emotions, and very personal and very real to me.

Though these are not originally in the Medicine Wheel, I have added in *Illustration 02* the term *attitudes* to the lake image as part of our personal makeup. My definition of an attitude is as follows: Our attitudes are our habitual ways of thinking, feeling and acting as we make our way through life. All this lies underneath our emotions.

Attitudes can be very positive and helpful. Jesus made attitudes the basis of his famous Sermon on the Mount, also known as the Beatitudes. These Beatitudes are "Ways of Being" in this world that help us realize the goal of his desired reign here on earth (Matthew 5:1-13). So attitudes are an important part of who we are, and will figure prominently in our exploration of functional and dysfunctional living. During a creative moment, I came up with a Twelve Step version of the Beatitudes that is included as an appendix at the end of this book.

Finally, the bottom of the lake represents the *spiritual*. In a sense, there is no bottom to us. We are always learning something new about ourselves, others, our Creator and life itself.

In the winter, lakes in many parts of Canada freeze over with a layer of ice that can be up to two metres thick. And so it is with many of us. The lack of love and the painful hurt we experienced as we grew up in dysfunctional families and societies created a layer of ice within us called fear. We have been hurt, and out of fear of even more pain, we close off, build invisible walls around ourselves, and swear that we will never let anyone hurt us again. Although that layer of ice insulates us from experiencing pain, we become hardened and isolated.

We especially fear *rejection* of our thoughts and feelings, that we will be laughed at and ridiculed if we are unmasked and others really know us. We fear the *unknown*, what it might be like if we ever broke through that protective wall of ice to let go of an addiction. We also resist *change*, as change is usually painful and also takes us into the unknown. Many of us are also afraid of the *truth*, especially the truth about ourselves. We are afraid that if people really got to know us they would not like us, as I had been afraid for years. In that sense, even though we yearn for intimacy, we fear it. Above all, we fear *abandonment*, the greatest fear a child has. And so, to our own detriment, we wall in our pain to protect ourselves from more pain, and set the stage for the need to medicate that pain through addictive behaviour.

To be fully human, we need to be in touch with that more personal part of ourselves: our thoughts, emotions and attitudes. To heal, we need to admit our thoughts, emotions and attitudes to ourselves, pray over them and share them with others. The challenge we face is to confront our fear of doing just that.

The Role of Thinking or Rational Intelligence

Without going into great detail here, as I want to keep the emphasis on emotions, I do want to include some ideas about thinking or rational intelligence. First, knowing our history helps us to not repeat it. Similarly, understanding what happened helps to heal our emotions. Also, what is blocked out, suppressed and unknown impedes healing. On the other hand, thinking positive thoughts can apparently influence the brain and help it to heal.

Remembering the past helps to express our feelings about the events. Connecting with the past also makes the abuse real, and knowing our past helps us to understand that our behaviour was more about what happened to us than about us. With these brief comments on the importance of thoughts in the healing process, we turn our attention now to the role of emotions.

The Importance of Emotions

Noted speaker and spiritual writer Sister Joan Chittister, O.S.B., points out the importance of expressing our emotions:

> The ability to express emotion is gift. Cut it off, throttle it at the source, trap it and it traps the person totally. Release it and the soul flies free. To suppress one emotion, in other words, is to suppress them all. Those who never know love will

never know joy either. Those who have never known pain can never go to the heights of happiness as well. Those who have stifled their own feelings cannot recognize, let alone release, the feelings of others. Chastity is not meant to stamp out the emotions. On the contrary, it is meant to direct them in ways that are magnanimous, in ways that are true, in ways that are freeing, in ways that are life giving. Emotions provide the fuel that guides us through life.[1]

For the purpose of simplicity, I want to point out that, in this book, I will be using the words "feelings" and "emotions" interchangeably, even though the word "emotions" touches a deeper reality that goes beyond the physical.

Here are a dozen gems of wisdom about emotions that I have gleaned over the years. They have been very useful to me on my own healing journey:

- Feelings are neither right nor wrong; they just are.

This teaching comes from the Marriage Encounter (M.E.) movement. I still remember the freeing impact that statement had on me as I walked into the conference room during my first Worldwide M.E. weekend and saw that poster on the wall. I began to realize, for the first time in my life at the age of 30, that feelings have no morality attached to them – they just are. It is okay to feel whatever I feel. That feeling is just a feeling, no matter how painful it might be, and it is only part of who I am at that moment.

The late Fr. John Monbourquette, O.M.I., echoes this teaching from Marriage Encounter in his writings:

> There is no emotion that is negative or shameful in itself. Emotions are made up of positive human energies that need to be recognized, controlled and put to good use. When feared or repressed by the subconscious, they form groups of emotions and images called "complexes" that then take on a life of their own. In Jungian psychology, repressed material forms the "shadow" side of one's personality that dominates uncontrollably as long as people refuse to notice it and try to

run away from it. If a person decides to slowly absorb their shadow, what may have seemed to be a destructive handicap will be transformed into energy and a source of personal and social growth.[2]

- Emotions are powerful energy in motion.

For John Bradshaw, a well-known speaker and writer on addictions, emotions are forms of powerful inner energy that must go somewhere, that must be expressed in some way. This energy is used to help us act effectively to take care of ourselves. Emotions are direct expressions of reality, as opposed to thoughts that translate or analyze our experience. "While our emotions are not all of who we are, they are our vital connection with life as it is now. Our emotions are one of our basic powers. They tell us of a need, loss or satiation. They are the oil-gauge on our car telling us how it goes with our basic needs. Such needs are the fuel without which our lives cannot run in any functional manner."[3]

Emotions give important information about what we want, how we need to change and what we need to do. As we shall see, they can be great motivators for getting those needs met. On the other hand, we can feel devastated when those needs are not met.

Some years ago, a 16-year-old girl from a northern community took her own life. She had left a note on her computer stating that she was smiling on the outside but screaming on the inside. Her inability to articulate her emotions, her inner silent scream, the inability of others to listen to her led her to act out of that emotion in a terrible, fatal way. Again, emotions are a powerful energy that must go somewhere, and all too often, the direction that those emotions take is self-destructive.

- Emotions are a gift from God, our Creator and Higher Power.

In First Nations spirituality, emotions are an integral component of the Medicine Wheel. We have been created to feel. To be human is to have feelings by God's design. To deny, suppress or ignore our emotions is to disrespect our God and to denigrate the awesome work of our Creator. Conversely, to acknowledge, own and honour

our emotions is to enter into the beauty and mystery of God's ongoing creative power.

- Emotions are a message from my inner child to my True Self.

During a reflective moment, I realized that an emotion is a message from my inner child to my True Self. I can learn from that emotion – learn more about myself, about life, about the Creator and about my place in the universe.

To my understanding, my True Self is the person that I am meant to be, "me" at my best, when I am balanced and well integrated. My inner child is the "me" with certain emotional needs that needed to be met as a child and still need to be met, even as an adult.

James Martin, S.J., in his book *My Life with the Saints,* states,

> Thomas Merton often distinguished between the "false self" and the "true self." The false self is the person we present to the world, the one we think will be pleasing to others: attractive, confident and successful. The true self, on the other hand, is the person we are before God. Sanctity consists in discovering who that person is and striving to become that person. As Merton wrote, "For me to be a saint means to be myself."[4]

In his *Seeds of Contemplation*, Merton adds, "Therefore the problem of sanctity and salvation is in fact the problem of finding out who I am and discovering my true self."[5]

Spiritual writer and storyteller John Shea tells a poignant story that touches on our True Self. It goes like this:

> When Rabbi Zusya grew old and knew that his time on earth was nearing a close, his students gathered around him. One of them asked him if he was afraid of dying. "I am afraid of what God will ask me," the Rabbi said. "What will he ask you?" they queried. "He will not ask me, 'Zusya, why were you not like Moses?' He will ask me, 'Zusya, why were you not Zusya?'"[6]

This story imparts the importance of knowing ourselves and of being true to ourselves, to be content as human beings and to bring Zusya home to Zusya.

- All emotions are positive, even though sometimes very painful.

If emotions are a gift from God and a message from my inner child to my True Self, it makes sense to state that there is no such thing as a "negative" emotion, that all emotions are positive, though sometimes very painful.

That understanding has helped me change my way of speaking about emotions. Like John Monbourquette, I no longer use the expression "negative emotions," and I feel some disappointment when I read authors who do. Instead, I use the words "pleasant" or "painful" as a personal preference.

As a scholastic brother in my last year of formation prior to being ordained, I yearned for a close relationship with the superior of our scholasticate (the equivalent of a seminary for religious congregations). Because I had not enjoyed a close relationship with my father, I saw the superior as a surrogate in my father's stead. While a closer relationship with the superior was my subconscious desire, I had no tools with which to accomplish this. I did not know how to relate to this father figure in a close, friendly manner. In fact, in his presence I would clam up, becoming tense, tongue-tied and very nervous.

At the same time, another scholastic with lots of charm was on a first-name basis with the superior, played tennis with him and enjoyed his company. The sight of them together would fill me with envy and jealousy. Not knowing how to deal with such painful emotions at that time of my life and thinking that I was not supposed to have feelings of jealousy as a scholastic, I denied and suppressed those feelings. Still, in the recesses of my heart, I felt guilty for harbouring those feelings that eventually flared up into a heated argument with that scholastic.

Only years later did I realize that the feeling of jealousy came out of the lack of love that I had experienced from my father. This jealousy was not a negative emotion, but rather a positive emotion, painfully trying to communicate to me that I had unmet emotional needs from my family of origin, and I needed to find healthy ways to have those needs met. Basically, this emotion was trying to tell me that I needed to heal my relationship with my father. Had I understood this much earlier in life, the wounded relationship with my father might have been healed much earlier. This would have given us more good years together before he died instead of the many tension-filled years that we experienced together, but apart.

I am convinced now that no matter how painful a feeling might be (depression, hatred, insecurity, suicidal despair, etc.), the feeling is positive, because it is part of being human. In the end, the statement that all feelings are positive is not simply naïve optimism, but rather a faith-filled stance towards the goodness of God's creation.

- Every emotion has an issue attached to it

Related to emotions as a lead into knowing our True Self is the insight that every emotion has an issue attached to it. For example, fear might relate to the unknown, anger to hurt, and sadness to loss. Our task is to understand and explore what the issue might be that is underlying each emotion, what message it carries, what we can learn from it, and how we can deal with it.

A pastor of a church was in therapy for sexually acting out. What puzzled him and his therapist was why he started acting out sexually after so many successful years in ministry. He was not close to his wife, nor to his parents. He did, however, have a close bond and intimate relationship with his paraplegic older brother, whom he had cared for but who had died.

The mystery was solved one day using the results of a Genogram exercise that was part of the program at this particular centre. A Genogram is basically a sketch of one's family tree, noting any addictions or problems through the generations. The therapist noticed that this pastor had started acting out sexually almost exactly a year after his brother died. He suggested that perhaps the reason for this behaviour was that, with the death of his brother, the pastor had lost the only intimacy he had in his life, and was now experiencing deep sadness, loss and loneliness. This awareness was the key to the pastor's healing. His unmet need for intimacy was the issue attached to the emotions he was feeling and to his resultant destructive behaviour.

The key for him to begin healing was to find ways to restore intimacy in his life once again.

- Suppression of emotions is emotional abuse.

Though the term *emotional abuse* can elicit rather violent images of put-downs and mind games, emotional abuse is rampant in our society and culture in many subtle ways. I have only to think back over my own experience and what my late mother used to say to us to realize that I unwittingly grew up with emotional abuse. I loved her very much, but now realize that she was a codependent adult child of an alcoholic. Speaking out of her own hurt, she was actually emotionally abusing us when she would say, "You shouldn't feel like that" (when I needed to feel those emotions) or "Everything is okay" (when it was not). Telling others not to feel, not to be free to be who they are at that moment, is to pressure them not to be human, and that is emotional abuse. This often happens at funerals, as well-meaning people admonish others to "be strong and don't cry."

Rhonda was a young adult participating in a Search for Christian Maturity weekend for youth. At one point in the program, the participants received a letter from their family and had an opportunity to respond. This was always an emotional moment. This particular time, I sensed hesitancy to express emotion within the group, so I stood in the centre of the room and announced that it was okay to cry if anyone needed to or felt like crying, that this was a safe place to express their feelings.

There was a moment of silence; then, suddenly, Rhonda broke out with a loud sob and rushed right past me into the girls' washroom. Later on, I asked her what that was all about. She shared with me that all her life she was told that she was the oldest, that she had to take care of her siblings and not to cry. When her mother died, she was told she had to be strong for their sake and not cry, so she did not allow herself to cry at her mother's funeral.

When she received the letter from her family that night and heard the words "It is safe to cry," it was like something broke inside of her; she just had to cry. I felt grateful. Rhonda had finally given herself permission to feel, to grieve, to mourn her loss, to cry, and that was a powerful healing for her. She had been emotionally abused as a youth, and in turn was emotionally abusing herself all those years.

Not only do we tell others to repress their feelings, we do this to ourselves. Realizing that denying our own emotions is self-inflicted emotional abuse is rather sobering and humbling. We need to be aware that, when we try to be strong and stoic, and counsel others to be the same, we may well be inflicting emotional abuse upon them and ourselves.

- Emotions deal with us if we don't deal with them.

If we don't acknowledge and in some way handle our emotions, we will act out of those emotions, and they will control us. Examples that illustrate this truth abound. A striking and very sad example is a young man who was not allowed by his friends to drive his car home from the local bar because he was drunk. When they arrived home, he took a baseball bat and, in a drunken rage, broke all the windows of his own car. He angrily asserted that if he could not drive it, no one else could either. Then, seconds before his stunned partner could react, he stormed into the house, grabbed a gun, and shot and killed himself.

I asked his sister after the funeral if she was aware of anything troubling him to bring about such devastating action. She told me that he had just recently insinuated to her that an uncle had sexually abused him as a child. I believe all that pain, held in for so long, led to not only his alcohol addiction but also to his rage and ultimately to his self-inflicted death.

Truly, emotions are a powerful energy that, if left repressed or unaddressed for too long, can affect us and others in terrible ways. If we don't deal with our emotions, they will deal with us, as we act out of the pain of those emotions.

- We transmit the pain we don't transform.

Good spirituality seeks to transform pain. This insight comes from Richard Rohr. So, too, does the opposite insight: that we transmit the pain we do not transform. The reality of so much horizontal or lateral violence in our families and in society today is actually the transmission of pain that has been repressed, suppressed or denied and often ends up being expressed against those closest to us, the ones we love.

The ability to act out of our pain lies within us all. In small or big ways, we can so easily lash out at others, unless we learn to transform our pain, especially by acknowledging and owning it, feeling it, praying about it and, above all, sharing it with others in safe ways. One young man, trying to deal with his alcoholism, used precisely those words: "When I drink, all those feelings go away, although I know I am just lashing out." The best antidote to violence is a strong spirituality that transforms it.

- We can't heal what we can't feel.

The key to healing is to start feeling the feelings. That is why, in therapy, clients will be counselled over and over again to feel the feelings, stay with the feelings, not run away from those feelings and, above all, share the emotions with others in counselling and in groups.

I remember a time when my own inability to identify my emotions affected my ministry and the ministry of others. Our group of northern pastoral ministers had just participated in a communications workshop with a facilitator to help us work together more effectively in ministry.

One of the main points she taught us was the importance of taking care of maintenance needs by sharing our feelings at the beginning of meetings. That round of sharing was a mechanism to free the participants to focus more effectively on the business to be conducted.

The facilitator ended the workshop by asking us to have a real-life planning meeting that she could observe. We embarked upon that, but immediately got stuck on a couple of issues; tempers flared and the meeting bogged down. Someone then remarked that we had neglected to start this meeting with a round of sharing. We stopped the business portion, and began to share the emotions we felt at that moment.

When the time came for me to share, I intellectualized something, but was cut short by another participant who accused me of being angry, which I immediately denied. I asked for more time, however, to sort out my emotions, and eventually realized that I *was* feeling angry. I was finally able to share that with the group.

Right after that round of sharing, the tone of the meeting changed, and synergy started to happen. The facilitator observed after the meeting that until we had the sharing round, our ideas were dropping into a void and evaporating into space, not connecting with each other at all. That changed dramatically, she pointed out to us, after our emotions had been shared.

In the end, although our thoughts and what is rational are important, the healing that we will experience will involve mostly the transformation of our emotions from painful to pleasant. Thus, a focus on emotions is critical to any healing process.

- We choose, and must own, our feelings.

It is a truism that no one can place feelings within us, or make us feel anything. As the *Al-Anon* book of daily meditations *One Day at a Time* puts it, "When I am pained by anything that happens *outside* of myself, it is not *that thing* which hurts me, but the way I think and feel about it" (January 7).

Many people fail to grasp this simple truth, and often blame others for how they feel, as evidenced by statements such as "You make me so mad." We can choose to cling to anger in all kinds of ways (denial, blame, refusing to forgive, repressing a feeling or nourishing it), only to have it emerge later on in more destructive ways. To heal, we have to choose to admit, deal with and let go of those painful emotions.

I believe that unidentified and unvalidated feelings are one of the roots of addiction. I also believe that a key to healing is to identify and to name the feelings. We must own them as our own. (In a sense, our feelings are the most personal possessions we have.) We must also choose to handle these emotions in a constructive way by sharing them with others, and then let them go, especially if they are painful emotions. We deserve to be free and to be free of them.

I remember journeying with a woman who had been terribly sexually abused by her own father. After one session during which she shared much of that painful experience, I felt an oppressive heaviness in my heart and literally experienced a weight on my shoulders. I knew I had to do something to deal with those emotions, or I would carry them for days, and they would affect me in all kinds of ways.

I chose to do two things. First, I wrote a letter to her father, sharing my emotions around what I had heard he had done to her. I sent her a copy to add to her letter to her father, should she ever choose to communicate her feelings with him. Then I chose to pray with those powerful, oppressive and heavy emotions. I sat in a chair and brought to mind, one by one, all the incidents of abuse that she had shared with me. I felt and named my emotions around each incident, put the images and emotions into imaginary garbage bags, tied an imaginary ribbon around the top of each bag and placed it at the foot of an imaginary cross with the prayer, "Lord, I heard it; now you carry it." At the end of that prayer session, I felt lighter and ready to move on. I had prayerfully processed my emotions around that abuse, and they would no longer control me.

- Sharing our feelings is one of the simplest and best ways to heal.

It is sometimes said that the most valuable things in life are free. It can also be said that one of the best ways to heal our painful emotions, that is, to share them, is free and simple as well. Much healing happens just by sharing our emotions with a trusted other, with a friend. I believe that a lot of therapeutic healing happens in marriages when spouses can talk over their problems and share their emotions honestly and openly with one another, or in relationships where people are soulmates with each other.

When we get to Step Six, we will see how this simple reality of honest sharing is at the heart of this step, and is very biblical as well. This process is so effective and powerful that it provides the major part of the healing involved at the core of the Twelve Step program, Steps Six and Seven. The nature of that healing will be dealt with in greater detail later in this book. Suffice it to say here that the simple process of identifying an emotion, staying with it instead of medicating it, expressing it through writing, or, better yet, sharing it with another human being, is a powerful way of freeing oneself from the destructive control that emotion potentially has.

There is a saying: "Grief shared is grief cut in half." I believe that the truth in this saying applies to all our painful emotions. There is a certain catharsis in the sharing of our emotions with others. We no longer carry them alone, and those that we still carry lose some of their intensity.

Marc Pizandawatc, co-founder of the Returning to Spirit program for healing the legacy of Indian residential schools, teaches that "withheld communication is the greatest cause of our upset." The opposite would then hold true – expressed emotions should be one of the most effective ways of achieving peace. Basically, painful emotions lose their power and control over us when shared, while pleasant emotions actually increase when they are shared.

In her novel *The Secret Life of Bees,* Sue Monk Kidd affirms this insight. After learning about May's hurting wall and her inability to handle pain, the main character in the novel, Lily, wonders,

> Did this mean if I told May about T. Ray's mounds of grits, his dozens of small cruelties, about my killing my mother – that hearing it, she would feel everything I did? I wanted to know what happened when *two* people felt it. Would it divide the hurt in two, make it lighter to bear, the way feeling someone's joy seemed to double it?[7]

The insight that, when shared, pleasant emotions actually increase is a positive note from which we can move on to address the issue of our human needs.

Our Basic Human Needs

According to the theory of *Reality Therapy,* by Dr. William Glasser, described in a presentation given in Saskatoon in the late 1970s, the basis of most problematic human behaviour is unmet human needs. He lists many of those needs: namely, love, survival (shelter, food, clothes), power, freedom, etc.

As these are probably familiar to most readers, for the purpose of this book I would like to expand only on the Love needs: to Be-Loved, to Be-Long, and to Be-Valued. These needs play a pivotal role in our psychological and spiritual makeup.

Our first and deepest human need, of course, is to *Be-loved*. I remember a call I received one day from a desperate woman whose husband was coming off a drunk. She pleaded for me to come over to talk to him. When I arrived at their home, he was sitting on the couch in the living room, surrounded by his wife and four children, who were quietly present in the house. They obviously all loved him and wanted him well and sober. Yet there he was, a big burly man, weeping and muttering, "Nobody loves me, nobody loves me."

It seems that he grew up in a very dysfunctional alcoholic home, and that his parents both froze to death because of drunkenness. Years later, with a family of his own, he was still unable to believe in or receive the love his family had for him, because the love he needed was not there for him as a child. Feeling unloved was the legacy he inherited, which proved to be the root of his own alcoholism and his inability to love and be loved throughout his life. John H. McGoey, author of the book *Through Sex to Love*, speaks of "emotional cripples" who are handicapped for life by feeling unloved. This alcoholic was one such cripple.[8]

Our second human need is to *Be-long*. For children, teenagers and adults, this is a powerful, ever-present need. How can words describe the fear we have as human beings of being rejected and left out? How much human suffering has been experienced from this need not being met in our formative childhood years, not to mention in our adolescent and adult stages of life? We need friends, people to do recreational activities with, hang out with, socialize with – groups to which we belong and where we feel accepted.

Those who are desperately seeking love will do almost anything to belong. A girl in a group home was being beaten and abused by members of a motorcycle gang. When asked why she hung around with these guys, she replied simply, "I have to belong somewhere."

Children, teenagers and adults will engage in behaviour ordinarily repugnant to them simply to belong and to be accepted.

A third human need is to *Be-valued*. We need to feel that we are important, that we matter and that we make a difference somehow, to someone, somewhere. Years of criticism, name calling, lack of love, lack of affection and lack of affirmation take their toll, and we begin to lose our sense of self-worth. Many people have great difficulty believing in their own worth.

God, our Creator, who is love, loves us unconditionally, giving us identity and dignity. We are children of God. We are entitled to respect; we are entitled to be valued – that is our right. That one's comments or position may not be valued does not devalue the essence of the individual.

One woman grew up believing she was stupid, because that was all she heard at home. It wasn't until, as an adult, she took a commercial cooking course with an exceptionally affirming instructor who repeatedly told her she could do it that she began to believe in herself. In fact, she blossomed, graduated with honours and carved out a successful career as a baker.

If we do not have a sense of our own self-worth, then life simply ceases to be worth living, and suicide becomes a real possibility. A young girl in a group home was caught flushing her medication down the toilet. When told that she needed the medication to live, she responded with a defiant "I don't care." She did not feel valued enough to hold her own life as important.

These needs to be beloved, to belong and to be valued are recognized by Gerald May, who expresses them in the following way: "… the fundamental spiritual longing that prompts people into this morass of psycho-spiritual confusion has three basic dimensions: a desire for unconditional love, a need for belonging and union, and a deep hunger to 'just be.'"[9]

People who have low self-esteem tend not to believe in the possibility of happiness and have a tendency to sabotage their desperate efforts to find some sense of self-worth. What a quandary a lack of self-worth puts many people into.

Fortunately, it doesn't have to be this way. There is an effective, concrete way to begin to have our needs met. This way is found in scripture, for there is a dynamic connection between the reality of our human needs and the Great Commandment of the Bible.

Human Needs and the Great Commandment

To my mind, the first and greatest psychologist has to be Jesus of Nazareth, because his teachings fit our human needs like a glove (quite understandably, since God created us).

One day a scribe came up to Jesus and asked him, "Which commandment is the first of all?"

He answered,

"Hear, O Israel: the Lord our God, the Lord is one; you shall love the Lord your God with all your heart, and with all your soul, and with all your mind, and with all your strength." The second is this, "You shall love your neighbour as yourself." There is no commandment greater than these. (Mark 12:28-34)

The answer takes the form of two commandments. The first, according to Jesus, is to *love God* with every fabric of our being. What Jesus is saying is that God loves us, and we are to love God in return. There is nothing you or I can do to make God love us more than God already does. All we have to do now is learn to love God back, and our deepest need to be loved will be met. We do this especially through prayer and worship.

The first part of the second commandment is to *love our neighbour*. What Jesus is saying here is that if we learn to really love others, to trust them, forgive them, care for them, accept them as they are, do good to them, even achieve intimacy with a select few soulmates, then we will start to belong to them, and our deep need to belong will be met.

The last part of the second commandment is to *love ourselves*. If we accept ourselves as we are, if we forgive ourselves our mistakes, if we learn to accept compliments, then our deep need to be valued will be met.

The Human Needs and Great Commandment can be matched up to make this more obvious:

Human Need: Great Commandment:

To Be-Loved   = Love God
To Be-Long   = Love your neighbour
To Be-Valued = Love yourself

Jesus knew our deepest human love needs, and he gave us a commandment that would ensure that those deep human needs would be met simply by living that teaching. When our human needs are met, we are on our way to being happy, free, sober human beings.

Met Needs

It is obvious from all that has been written above that having our needs met is crucial for our well-being as human beings. While using scripture is one way to start fulfilling that need, the question that remains to be answered is how our needs can be met in other ways.

Some of the ways that those needs can be met in families are through expressed affection; being listened to and heard; being blessed and affirmed; sharing, validating and respecting feelings; sharing family activities and praying together; along with providing discipline and guidance.

Though this list is certainly not exhaustive, hopefully it will serve as a stimulus for the reader to develop his or her own list particular to his or her situation, as a way of ensuring that children's emotional needs are met. All these practices are simply a means of living out that Great Commandment of Jesus and of providing the love that young people need. These met needs will equip children for the hard knocks that life will present them. They will be able not only to survive but also to successfully negotiate the pitfalls of life and to avoid the trap of addictions.

In the process of exploring the importance of met and unmet needs, it would be helpful to study how we operate as human beings with the help of an image based on the Medicine Wheel that I call the *Awareness Wheel*.

Our *Vision* (senses/sensations) takes in information about different events around us. These sensations are perhaps the most basic information we can garner about ourselves and the world. To become aware of these sensations and to attend to them requires a great degree of *mindfulness*. A friend informed me that Buddhism is particularly strong in this area. This information is then filtered through our *Belief System*. This belief system is made up of our thoughts, judgments, decisions, memories, understanding, conscience, intuition and imagination. We interpret our reality in all these ways.

The Awareness Wheel

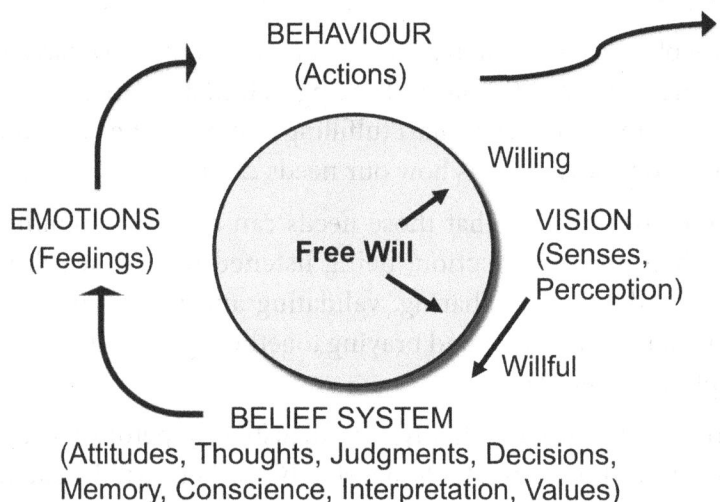

Illustration 03

All of these human functions influence our feelings and *emotions*. Underneath our belief system and our feelings and emotions are our *attitudes* that, as we have seen, are our habitual ways of thinking and feeling about things and about life. All this in turn has an influence on our *actions*, on how we behave on a day-to-day basis.

It is affirming to find authors who concur with one's ideas, articulating them in a similar manner. Ksenijaa Napan states, "Our experience of life is dependent on our perception. Our perception is dependent on our thoughts. Our quality of life is dependent on the quality of our thoughts and we are the only ones who can control them. This implies that thoughts and perceptions shape our experience of reality."[10]

Gerald May, in his book *Will and Spirit*, explains that at the centre of this circle is our free will. That is the great human gift from the Creator – the ability to choose how we will live our lives. We can either be *willful* and stubbornly insist on living life according to our own terms, our own will (which usually results in addiction), or we can be *willing* and open to respond to the movement of God's Spirit gently calling to us, at our deepest level of being, to do God's will, which leads to happy, free sobriety. The Big Book describes being *willful* in these stark terms: "So our troubles, we think, are basically of our own making, and the alcoholic is an extreme example of self-will run riot, though he doesn't usually think so."[11]

As May puts it so succinctly, "Whenever one mires down in a willful attempt to master life, the strongest feeling encountered is loneliness. It is impossible to be truly, intimately close to anything or anyone when one is either controlling or being controlled." On the other hand, he states, "willingness implies a surrendering of one's self-separateness, an entering into, an immersion in the deepest processes of life itself."[12]

The Wellness Wheel of Met Needs

The Wellness Wheel combines the reality of emotions and met human needs. This is a concise way of describing and understanding how healthy human beings operate. Human needs followed by belief systems flow into emotions. Those emotions lead to behaviours undergirded by our attitudes.

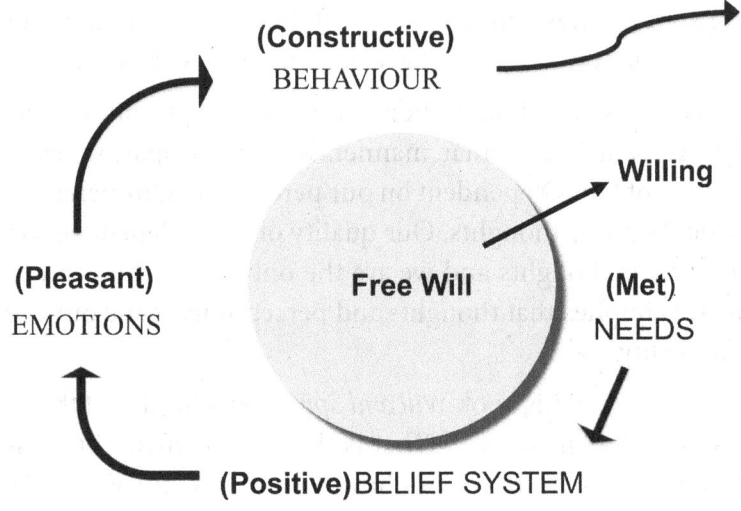

Illustration 04

When our human needs are met, a positive belief system is developed, leading to positive thoughts, perceptions of the world as a friendly place, and positive decisions making informed, correct judgments. Our emotions will tend to be pleasant ones, such as happiness, peace, joy, freedom and contentment. Our behaviour will tend to be constructive actions that contribute in a positive way to the building up of our lives, families and society. We will basically go through life, and be seen by others, as someone with a positive attitude.

Though not as clear cut as depicted in *Illustration 04*, and with some back-and-forth interaction, the movement within the circle, as in the Medicine Wheel, tends to be clockwise (met needs, positive belief systems, pleasant emotions and, finally, constructive behaviour).

Observing children can teach us much in this area of met needs. I remember a family Christmas gathering where we were opening presents, chatting and generally enjoying ourselves after a traditional supper of turkey and all the fixings. One of my nieces, about six years old at the time, came up to me, all smiles, holding a newly opened toy, and unabashedly proclaimed, "Uncle, everybody loves me!"

That one quick statement from this young child struck a deep, responsive chord within me. Immediately I recognized that she was living within the Wellness Wheel. Her human needs to be loved, to belong and to be valued were met, and she had a very positive belief system. She believed that she was loved and loveable. As a result, her emotions were very pleasant feelings of self-esteem, self-assurance and enjoyment of life. And of course, her actions were appropriate, constructive and a positive contribution to the life of her family. Years later, as a young adult, she continues to demonstrate these same qualities.

There are certainly many other ways that our human needs to be loved, to belong and to be valued can be met. Meeting them should be the goal of all family life. We will see in Parts Four and Five how the Twelve Step program addresses those needs. The Awareness Wheel and the Wellness Wheel we have just looked at are models that serve as a background to working the Twelve Step program.

We turn now to exploring a spirituality of recovery and wellness in Part Two.

Suggested Activities

1. Start a journal to record your reflections and emotions throughout the reading of this book.
2. Create your own personal timeline as a line going upwards. Mark off segments in the timeline representing five-year periods. Identify significant events throughout your life and place them on your timeline.
3. Pray with your timeline: What were the physical events, the intellectual events, the emotional events and the spiritual events?

QUESTIONS FOR REFLECTION

Journal your answers to the following questions:

1. Who are the significant people who have made a difference in your life?
2. What were the major challenges you had to face and perhaps are still addressing?
3. What growth or setbacks did you experience in your life as a result?
4. What do you need to put into place to move forward in your life?

PART TWO: A Spirituality of Recovery and Wellness

Before delving into the journey leading to addiction, and from that into the Twelve Step healing journey, it will be helpful to be grounded in the realm of spirituality. In this section, we will explore a broad spectrum of spiritualities involved in the process of recovery and wellness, first as a way of better understanding the dynamics of addiction and then as a way of preparing the ground for the more specific Twelve Step healing journey.

An Integrated Spirituality

One of the aims of this book, and part of its richness, is to integrate First Nations, Twelve Step and Christian spirituality. This is not something new, as it is based on the first paragraph of the Apostles' Creed that has been prayed since antiquity. In the first part of that prayer, we say, "I believe in God the Father (*Christian spirituality*), Almighty (*Twelve Step spirituality*), Creator (*First Nations spirituality*) of heaven and earth." There we have it – God who is Father, Higher Power and Creator. As you may already be aware, this integrated spirituality will be apparent throughout this book.

Definitions of Spirituality

Much could be written about the vast panorama of spirituality. To keep our focus on recovery and wellness, I will offer here four brief, incisive insights into spirituality, followed by what I have found to be the most helpful definition of spirituality to date in terms of living a fully human life free from addiction.

1. *Spirituality is all about what we do with our pain.*

This definition comes from Richard Rohr. Along with his previous insight into transmitting the pain we don't transform, he provides an interesting glimpse into spirituality with this one phrase about dealing with pain. The pain that we speak of here is the suffering that we endure from carrying within us intense, dark emotions, such as anger, hatred, bitterness and fear.

It doesn't take much reflection to realize that addiction is all about avoiding pain, running away from pain, medicating pain and numbing our painful emotions. Spirituality is just the opposite – it confronts pain and deals with it. A strong spirituality will deal with pain and transform it; a weak spirituality will try to avoid pain. The best antidote to horizontal violence is a strong spirituality that deals with pain.

Sometimes in counselling or therapy, one will hear phrases such as "No pain, no gain" or "The only way through the pain is through the pain." These are not simply glib phrases – they carry much wisdom and articulate some of that spirituality.

2. *Spirituality is all about letting go.*

This definition of spirituality also comes from Rohr, who says,

> All great spirituality is about letting go. Instead, we have made it be about taking in, attaining, performing, winning and succeeding. Spirituality has become a show we perform for ourselves, which God does not need. True spirituality mirrors the paradox of life itself. It trains us in both detachment and attachment – detachment from the passing so we can attach to the substantial. But if you do not acquire good training in detachment, you may attach to all the wrong things, especially your own self-image and its desire for security. Self-interest becomes very well disguised, often passing for religion.[13]

So, spiritually speaking, addiction has a lot to do with attachment. Our natural tendency, because of past hurts and lack of love, is to cling to things, events and persons that end up harming us. A healthy spirituality is just the opposite – it is all about letting go. To heal, we need to let go. We must let go of painful emotions such as anger, resentment, sadness and grief. We must let go of defects of character such as false pride, stubbornness, control and impatience. Above all, we must let go of our addictions, our habitual abuse of the gifts of creation such as alcohol, drugs, food and money, as well as harmful activities such as excessive gambling, destructive gossip and irresponsible sex.

3. *Spirituality is a transformative journey.*

It has been said that life is more a journey than a destination. For one writer on spirituality, James Finley, life is a long, often arduous journey on which we slowly become detached from our false, illusory self, a self that is little more than the collective evaluations and affirmations of our surroundings, and are opened up to receive a new self that is participation in the life of God and an inner transformation of our personalities.[14] Finley asserts that the whole of our spiritual life finds its fulfilment in bringing our entire life into a loving, transforming union with the ineffable God. It is a journey in which we discover ourselves in discovering God, and discover God in discovering our True Self, hidden in God.

God is continually creating, and therefore every day is miraculous.[15] The language of God is what God writes into human experience. As spiritual human beings, we are constantly on a journey, in process, healing and growing. I believe it was Cardinal John Henry Newman who articulated the profound observation that "To live is to change, and to live well is to have changed much." Truly, life is a journey of transformation.

4. *Spirituality is all about relationships.*

We have seen how one of our deepest human needs is for belonging, or fellowship. We will see shortly how pivotal that reality is in our lives. As human beings, our relationships are four-fold: 1) our relationship with God or Higher Power; 2) our relationship with others; 3) our relationship with ourselves; and 4) our relationship with all of God's creation.

How true it is that no one is an island. Even those who choose to live alone or live the lifestyle of a monk are social beings. Thomas Merton, a Trappist monk, touched and influenced the lives of thousands from his solitude by his writings, his prayer and his spirituality. Spirituality is all about the relationships that we maintain in our lives, as evidenced in the following section on Teepee Spirituality.

Teepee Spirituality

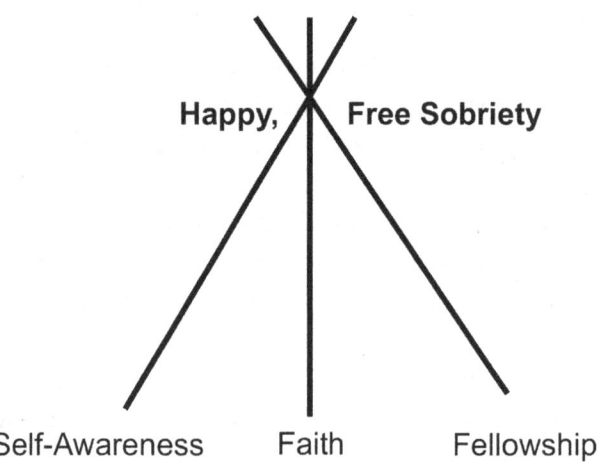

Illustration 05

One of the key values and concepts of First Nations spirituality is the idea of living in harmony and balance with oneself, with the Creator and with all of creation. This model of Teepee Spirituality emerged over the years from pondering and experiencing the power and beauty of First Nations thought and spirituality, and has proved to be helpful in counselling people with addictions. It has also come from the experience of owning a teepee and setting it up, which invariably draws a crowd of helpful onlookers – I have never set it up alone. Once up, it provides a warm, safe, secure home-like space, conducive for sharing or just relaxing.

The first step in setting up a teepee involves erecting a tripod with three poles. No pole can stand alone, nor can two. Three poles are needed for a structure to be strong enough to stand on its own, firm and stable.

Our lives are the same. Human beings need three poles upon which we can build lives of happy, free sobriety. These three poles are Faith (prayer), Fellowship (friendship), and Self-awareness (self-worth). No one pole in our lives can stand on its own.

1. The Pole of Faith

The first pole is *Faith* expressed in prayer. We need deep faith in a Higher Power and "conscious contact" with that Higher Power through prayer, ceremonies and worship. Yet prayer, while good in itself, is not enough. Prayer by itself can become an escape from dealing with our pain and can even become an addiction when isolated and on its own. This is especially dangerous for those whose faith background tends to be individualistic ("me and God" or "me and Jesus") and not rooted in a faith community.

Some people believe that if they pray hard enough, loud enough and long enough, they will feel different, and often they do. The danger in doing this, however, is the very real possibility of religious addiction. We must ask the hard question: Is this really prayer and deep spirituality, or simply medicating one's pain (the goal of addiction), only by means of religion? One can very easily get off balance and hurt others as well as delay one's own progress in sobriety, if faith, prayer or religion becomes isolated, individualistic, escapist and addictive. We will see an example of this reality later.

2. The Pole of Fellowship

The second pole of the teepee foundational tripod is *Fellowship* or friendship, relationship and sharing. To balance faith and prayer, we need relationship with others, based on mutual trust and acceptance. We need to share our True Selves with others and to hear them share with us who they really are. We yearn for and need to experience intimacy in our lives, to speak our truth and to hear the truth from others. As we have seen, one of our deepest human needs is for belonging. It is fellowship that grounds us in relationships and meets that deep human need.

Many people trying to recover hamper their own progress due to a lack of understanding of the importance of fellowship. As a result, they often and quite quickly begin to miss their support group meetings after sobering up, or after leaving a treatment centre, rendering themselves very vulnerable to relapse.

The best form of fellowship happens at support group meetings where persons share their feelings about the steps they are working, especially Steps Four to Nine. Working those steps sincerely will involve going deep, remembering hurtful events and destructive reactions to them, feeling the pain of anger, resentment, sadness, shame, grief, guilt and fear all over again. Now, however, we are ready to let go of those painful emotions and to deal with them by sharing that pain with others who will hear us, who will remember what we share and, above all, accept us without comment and with compassion and empathy. This is the love that heals.

It is here that the rubber hits the road. There is room for some "drunk-a-logues," as people entertain others with stories of what they were like and the things they did back in their drinking days, but there is a danger of staying there, hiding behind the humour and never getting to the point where they share their feelings about the steps they are working on. Never getting to this point leads some people to quit the meetings in frustration, claiming that all they hear are the same stories over and over.

The challenge is always to share one's feelings about the step one is working on; this kind of sharing is always fresh and exciting, and never repetitious. At the same time, it is always a bit frightening, because it demands raw courage, rigorous honesty, trust and vulnerability – the stuff that love is made of. How true it is that we crave love, yet fear it as well. Hopefully, understanding fellowship as trust and acceptance, both deep forms of love, will encourage all who read these words to dare to enter into the experience of genuine healing fellowship.

A significant and formative experience of fellowship happened to me when I joined the A.A. group in Beauval in 1976. For a year, I had attended the weekly meetings faithfully out of a sense of duty as a pastor. In that role, I would share a brief spiritual talk at the end of each meeting. At the same time, my agenda, my need to fix things, my workaholism and people pleasing were putting an increasingly heavy inner burden and stress on me. I felt a constant tension in my stomach and probably a low-grade depression in my spirit, though I kept a smile on my face. Once in a while, I would overhear a comment like "Father is burning the candle at both ends," but I dismissed this as merely misinformed opinion.

More and more, at each A.A. meeting, however, I found myself envying the members – envying their laughter, their fellowship, their joking around over coffee after the meetings, basically, their happiness, which so often obviously exceeded mine. Though I denied and buried it at the time (after all, I was their pastor, there to help them), often I felt sad, burdened, tense and angry. I had years of intellectual formation, but I was totally unaware of my defects of character and my addictions, and had no idea of my need for healing. How could I help others until I was aware I had issues and had started to deal with them?

Thank God the joy, freedom and happiness in the group worked on me, meeting after meeting. I marvel now at how patient they were, listening to their young pastor expound about things spiritual, totally from the head and from books, probably without connecting with their lived reality at all. In the end, I wanted what they had, and I asked the chairperson if I could join the group. He replied, "Sure, lots of people work the program for themselves even though they aren't alcoholics."

Even with that invitation, it took me three weeks to work up the courage to share at a meeting, because to join the group would mean telling my story and sharing my feelings, instead of giving a spiritual talk. I was scared and fearful they might reject me as a priest if I revealed to them that I was not "perfect" and that I was struggling with personal issues. I was caught in that ice of fear in the Lake of our Humanity that we discussed in Part One. But some mysterious inner force kept nudging me on.

I desperately wanted to join, and finally did so at one meeting. I'll never forget that experience. When invited to speak, I introduced myself as a friend of alcoholics, said I wanted to join the program, took a deep breath and proceeded to share with them my personal problems and my painful emotions that I was struggling with at the time.

We then stood up to pray the Lord's Prayer. After that prayer, I stood frozen in uncertainty, not daring to look up, knees trembling and arms limp at my side. Then I felt someone shake my hand, and someone else put a cup of coffee in my hand.

Those two silent gestures were powerful. Suddenly, I was almost overwhelmed with a sense of belonging, acceptance and relief. I was in! I belonged to the group. What a feeling of love that was. That experience has helped me understand the power of fellowship.

In 1 Corinthians 13:4-9, St. Paul describes love as many things. In some translations, he ends this description with two words that I think summarize love best in terms of the program: "Love is always ready to *trust* and to *accept* whatever comes." Trust and acceptance are what love is all about. That trust and acceptance, that love, is what I experienced powerfully that night I joined the program.

As I reflected on that experience, I began to understand more about the nature of fellowship, how fellowship works, and how important it is to a life of sobriety. *Illustration 06*, showing me in the middle of the diagram, is an attempt to visualize what happened to me that night.

When I shared my personal thoughts and painful feelings, I trusted the group and they felt it. That was love. The participants simply listened and, without making any comment or reaction, took into their hearts the pain and the reality that I was sharing. There was no crosstalk. They accepted me as I was, without judging or evaluating. Fellowship is love at a deep level, expressed as trust and acceptance of our fellow human beings. It is this experience of love that heals.

Fellowship = Love and Intimacy

Love as

Trust and

Acceptance

(1 Corinthians 13:7)

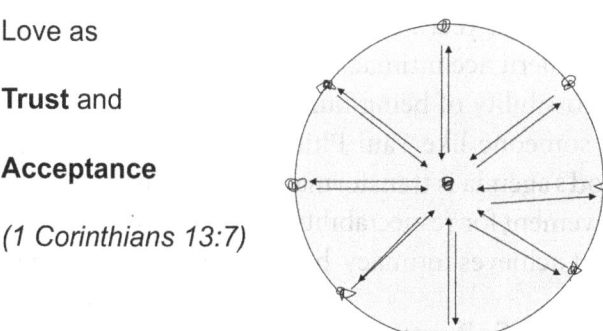

Illustration 06

I have since heard from others who have had a similar experience. One person shared with me what it was like for her to open up for the first time to a group. She said that it became very quiet – no one else made a sound. I explained to her that the group could tell that she was going deep, opening up, baring her soul, and so they became very quiet. That was a sacred moment. They sensed and felt her trust in them, her love for them, and it is that love that heals.

This person also said that it seemed like time stood still during her sharing. I explained to her how this made sense also, since with God, there is no time (2 Peter 3:8). She was experiencing God as love by trusting others as she did, and experiencing that depth of acceptance. It was a God-moment, an experience of the Kingdom of God, and time became irrelevant. We were both quite moved by her experience that deepened our appreciation of fellowship in the program.

Jean Vanier, son of the former Governor General of Canada and founder of the L'Arche homes for people with and without disabilities, captured the essence of fellowship in one of his talks, which I attended some years ago: "When we are humble, honest and open enough to share our weakness and brokenness with our brothers and sisters, that frees them to be humble, honest and open enough to share their weakness and brokenness with us, and together we grow." That is genuine, healing fellowship.

At its deepest level, fellowship is all about experiencing intimacy in our lives. We all yearn for intimacy, yet fear it at the same time, because to experience intimacy, we must be vulnerable, opening us up to the possibility of being hurt again. Yet the risk is well worth taking, as someone like Paul Philibert expresses so well when he writes, "God's agenda is transformation through intimacy, not moral self-improvement for respectability."[16] Fellowship, and especially fellowship that achieves intimacy, has a transformative power.

3. The Pole of Self-awareness

The third pole of Teepee Spirituality is *Self-awareness*. This is perhaps the most difficult area of the three. Shakespeare's famous statement "Would that we could see ourselves as others see us" certainly applies here.

A team of Jesuits were presenters at a conference years ago. They left the participants with one key phrase: "religious awareness." Many good people, perhaps our parents, the presenters claimed, did not grow personally, simply because they were never taught the skills of self-awareness and had no way to access or express their emotions. Perhaps many of us were raised the same way, taught to repress feelings and thoughts and to distrust others.

Sometimes in ministry, I encounter people who are running away from the painful truth about themselves and who can't heal or change. I heard recently of a gifted person who had initiated a renewal program that helped hundreds of people grow personally. I was shocked to hear that after a few years, his colleagues and the board of directors had to do an intervention on him because of his addiction to alcohol. He resisted and even tried to garner support for himself from former participants of the program. I don't know what the eventual outcome was or how messy the process became, but I was struck by the deep-seated need we have to preserve our false selves, even to our own detriment.

We would sooner condemn ourselves to that invisible prison of our false selves than risk finding out that we are loving and loveable. I suspect that for people to be able to receive painful personal feedback and truly see themselves as they are would be a bigger miracle than the quick fixes that some seem to be seeking, even at faith gatherings.

My journey into greater self-awareness began during spiritual direction at the scholasticate with then Fr. Adam Exner, O.M.I. In our first session, he asked me to tell him my story. "What story?" I asked, not knowing what he meant. He invited me to tell him about my life, starting as far back as I could remember. Once I got started, I talked for over two hours through two sessions. At the end of my sharing, he shared with me the observation that I needed to work on my relationship with my father, and asked me to pray with the scripture passage from Isaiah 43:1-7 for a month. That passage included the sentence "I regard you as precious, since you are honoured and I love you."

Those sessions and that passage had a great impact on me. After all those years of trying to earn my father's love, I now heard God our Father speaking words of love to me – that I was precious and honoured in God's sight, not because of anything I had done, but simply because God loved me. I can honestly say that this was the beginning of my lifelong healing journey.

Our fledgling attempts at building basic Christian community in Beauval with the Grey Nuns and a friend who had moved in with me to experience community life led to another momentous occasion of self-awareness for me.

When canoeing one day, a couple of months after we had initiated our little community, I asked this friend how he saw me. He asked me if I really wanted to know. I responded that yes, I was ready for any feedback that he might give me. Had I known what he was going to say, I might not have asked. He replied that, from his experience of me over the past months, I did not know how to live, I did not know how to love, I was always trying to prove something and I had not accepted myself as I was.

I almost fell out of the canoe, so shocked was I by this sudden painful yet truthful reflection of me coming from a friend who truly knew me. I breathed deeply, recouped and, surprisingly, kept on paddling without putting up too much resistance. He must have caught me on a good day. I did, however, do some pretty serious reflection, prayer and adjusting after that revelatory moment.

I believe that feedback from this friend was part of the mix that led me to join the Alcoholics Anonymous program in Beauval later that fall. After joining A.A. I was invited to give lectures on spirituality at the rehabilitation centre in Île-à-la-Crosse. I began to work the program, and I dealt with quite a few other defects of character that surfaced along the way – defects such as impatience, stubbornness and control, to name a few.

These three indispensable poles of Teepee Spirituality come together at the top and form a strong foundational structure for our teepee of happy, free sobriety. They are always and everywhere interrelated and joined together. In self-awareness, we learn who we are, and can share this with others in fellowship. In fellowship, we affirm others, receive feedback from them and learn more about who we are. In prayer, we share all of this with God and become even more aware of who we are in God's eyes. Ideally, all three (Faith, Fellowship and Self-awareness) come together and work together, especially in deep, healing moments of shared prayer.

Teepee Spirituality, Human Needs and the Great Commandment

In terms of Teepee Spirituality, you may already have noticed the connection of the three poles (Faith, Fellowship and Self-Awareness) with the three human needs discussed in Part One – the need to Be-Loved, to Be-Long, and to Be-Valued, and the Great Commandment given to us by Jesus.

The first pole, Faith or prayer, connects with our need to be loved. The one who loves us first, of course, is God, who is love. The second pole, Fellowship or friendship, connects with our need to belong. The more we can enter into deep fellowship with our fellow human

Part Two: A Spirituality of Recovery and Wellness

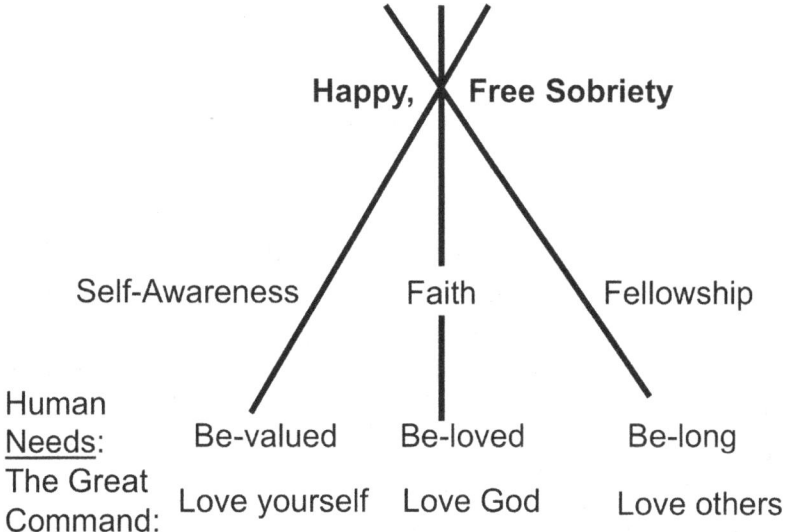

Illustration 07

beings, the more our need to belong will be met. The third pole, Self-awareness, connects with our human need to be valued, to have self-worth and self-esteem. As we have already seen, the ability to feel, identify and validate our feelings is perhaps the most basic way of knowing ourselves, of being aware of who we are at that moment.

The last part of the Great Commandment is to love ourselves, or as it is stated, to love our neighbours as we love ourselves. It is difficult to love our neighbours, or God, if we do not love ourselves, if we believe deep down that, when it comes to us, God made junk. No, God does not make junk, and we are asked to integrate that belief deep within our own personalities.

Another of my nieces demonstrated that sense of self-assurance and sense of being loved at the early age of five. It was obvious from the start that she was exceptionally gifted with a command of words. She delighted in reciting lines memorized from songs, such as "Supercalifragilisticexpialidocious," from the movie *Mary Poppins*. One day, she showed me how much she had saved in her piggy bank. I decided to test her ability with words, so I commented that she was a very "frugal" little miss. I was certain that would stump her. She gave me a puzzled look for a few seconds, then said simply, "Thank you," and walked away. To this day I don't know if she understood or not, and I was the one who was stumped. It is hard to faze a child, a teen, even an adult, or anyone who knows they are loved.

Negatively, the inability to love ourselves or to see our own self-worth manifests itself in a tendency to reject compliments. A vivid and rather painful memory of an incident that happened to me will serve as an illustration. Back in 1976, before I joined A.A., I was attending a priest's retreat. I was walking outside with a friend during a break when we encountered a brother Oblate. He looked up, smiled and greeted me with a friendly "Gee, Sylvain, it's good to see your face again." Instantly, and without thinking, I blurted out, "Sure, if you've got nothing better to look at." He was visibly taken aback, a hurt look flashed across his face, and he said abruptly, "I do, every time I look in a mirror," as he continued on his way.

I felt confused, small and embarrassed, and wanted to crawl under the pavement. Why had I said that? What was wrong with me? Where did that comment come from? It took some time before I stopped beating myself up for that comment, a comment that certainly took the joy out of that retreat. Now, of course, I realize that at that time, even as an educated and ordained priest in charge of a mission, I was struggling with low self-worth. I did not believe I was worthy of such love from another human being, and I pushed it away instinctively. I needed healing from low self-worth, a healing that thankfully has happened over the years. I can now accept compliments. I have learned to say "Thank you," though it was not easy, took some time and is an ongoing challenge to this day.

As these examples illustrate, loving ourselves, being loved, and being able to love others are intertwined in our lives. How the Great Commandment given to us by Jesus connects with the Teepee model of spirituality can provide deeper insights into this intriguing dimension of human life.

A time when Teepee Spirituality, Met Human Needs and the Great Commandment came together in my life was early in my ministry at Beauval. After the sisters and I had experienced our first World Wide

Marriage Encounter, we began to trialogue every Friday night. We would lock the door, go upstairs in the convent, gather around the circular oak table there and do something we called "night sharing," which I had learned from Fr. Armand Nigro, S.J., on a 30-day retreat.

We would first pray a psalm and share a word from the scriptures that struck us. This was a form of faith sharing. Then we would share our feelings and emotions. This was not easy at first, but we got better at it as we went along. Third, we would share our personal needs, and pray for each other's needs. This would be a very simple prayer for courage, strength, hope, serenity, whatever need the other expressed. Finally, we would play a game of Uno or cards.

That experience of intentional and warm community life, an experience of faith, fellowship and self-awareness, was instrumental in our growth, healing and personal transformation. This, along with other programs such as the Christopher Leadership Course, had such a healing effect on one of the sisters, who stuttered and was very shy, that she lost her stutter and gained the confidence to lead the singing in the church. Her religious community was amazed at the transformation in this sister.

A Spirituality of Human Incompleteness

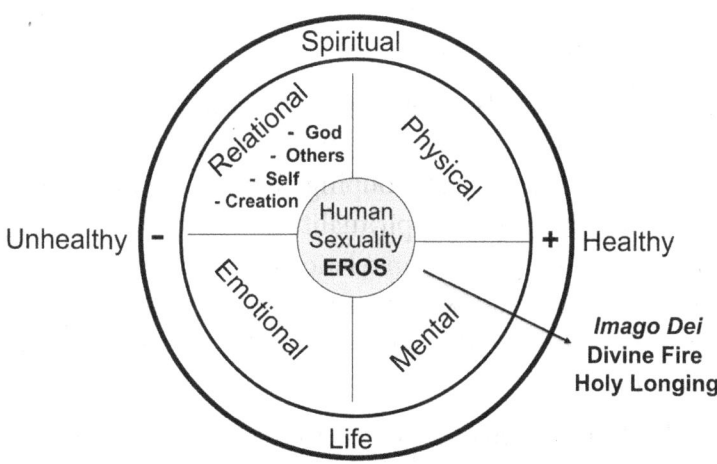

Illustration 08

The four definitions of spirituality presented earlier are offered as an insightful glimpse into the fascinating and profound world of spirituality. Some common ideas about spirituality come from classic mysticism, Eastern mysticism and First Nations spirituality. Many writers present spirituality as being somewhat esoteric, out of the ordinary and exclusive, an all-too-common impression held by the ordinary person on the street. In so doing, these writers misrepresent the central issue that spiritual life is about the ordinary. Everyone has a spiritual life, good or poor. Spiritual life is about living out our common humanity.

There is, therefore, a need for a more holistic, simple understanding of spirituality. The definition of spirituality below can help people see themselves as spiritual persons having a human experience. I have adapted this definition that comes in large part from Oblate theologian and spiritual writer Ron Rolheiser who in turn draws upon his interpretation of the writings of St. John of the Cross. The definition is as follows:

"Spirituality is the tension of living positively our human incompleteness."

Illustration 08 will help us unpack this dynamic view of spirituality. This image once again draws on the wisdom of the Medicine Wheel. The first three parts, as usual, are the Physical, Mental (intellectual) and Emotional.

The wheel then adds an unexpected fourth part, the Relational or social. Recall one of our deepest human needs: to belong, to have friends, to be part of a social grouping, to have relationships. Recall also the earlier definition of spirituality as being all about relationships. As mentioned, our human relationships encompass four levels: a relationship with God who created us, relationships with other people, a relationship with ourselves and, lastly, a relationship with all of creation.

The illustration then takes another rather intriguing and surprising turn towards the centre of the circle, but also towards the centre of our being as humans, and that is our Human Sexuality, or "Eros," a term that begs explanation.

To complete the illustration, the outer circle shows that how we live all these factors, positively or negatively, *is* our Spiritual Life. Perhaps it is clearer now that we are all spiritual persons, and that all of us, saint and sinner alike, have a spiritual life. The key determination is whether we are living our spiritual life positively or negatively.

Let us now plunge into a deeper exploration of this evocative illustration that defines spirituality as "living positively the tension of our human incompleteness."

As Rolheiser states in his book *The Holy Longing*, paraphrasing a phrase attributed to Plato, "We are fired into life with a madness that comes from the gods and which would have us believe that we can have a great love, perpetuate our own seed, and contemplate the divine." Rolheiser continues,

> Everyone is ultimately talking about the same thing as unquenchable fire, a restlessness, a longing, a disquiet, a hunger, a loneliness, a gnawing nostalgia, a wildness that cannot be tamed, a congenital all-embracing ache that lies at the centre of human experience and is the ultimate force that drives everything else. This dis-ease is universal. Desire gives no exemptions.[17]

In other words, we experience the tension of incompleteness on all levels of our being. Although that "inchoate longing" is difficult to pinpoint or describe, it has been written about throughout the history of humanity. This longing has found a variety of expressions over the ages in songs, movies, writing and art. Philosophers speak of "part of a whole." The Greeks spoke of *nostos*, of homesickness. Gerard Manley Hopkins called the human spirit an "imprisoned skylark." Augustine said, "You have made us for yourself, Lord, and our hearts are restless until they rest in you." Country singer kd Lang's popular song "Constant Cravings" is a more contemporary expression of that longing.

A poignant expression of this "longing" is found in the diary of Anne Frank:

> The sun is shining, the sky is a deep blue, there is a lovely breeze and I am longing so, longing for everything: to talk, for

freedom, for friends, to be alone. And I do so long ... to cry! I feel as if I am going to burst, and I know that it would get better with crying; but I can't, I am restless, I go from room to room, breathe through the crack of a closed window, feel my heart beating, as if it is saying, "Can't you satisfy my longing at last?" I believe that it is spring within me; I feel that spring is awakening; I feel it in my whole body and soul. It is an effort to behave normally, I feel utterly confused. I don't know what to read, to write, what to do, I only know that I am longing.[18]

Daniel O'Leary, a pastor and spiritual writer, expressed this same longing in these words:

There is an existential longing that never stops nagging at our human soul. A lust to live life to the full, to love like the greatest lovers, courses relentlessly in our bloodstreams. Everything about us is constantly tinged with an incessant yearning for some indefinable reality. This raw and relentless compulsion to transcend our own mortality is the restlessness of the indwelling Holy Spirit, drawing us towards the heart of God. As Robert Browning wrote, "Ah! But a man's reach must exceed his grasp, or what's a heaven for?"[19]

The explanation for this deeply felt angst of being human, according to Rolheiser, is another insight – that spirituality is an erotic urge, a statement that needs some explanation.[20]

There is a reason why human sexuality and "Eros" is at the centre of our Medicine Wheel illustration. The first question asked when we were born is usually, "Is it a boy or a girl?" We are an "it" until that is established, and that is about as basic as it gets. That question is a question of gender, of human sexuality. Recall the words of scripture: "God created humans in the image of himself, in the image of God he created them, male and female God created them" (Genesis 1:27).

An Internet check reveals that the word "sex" is derived from the Latin word *sexus*, meaning "quality of being either male or female." It is commonly taken with *seco* as "division" or "half" of the race, which would connect it to *secare*, "to divide, cut off or section." Thus, when a chainsaw cuts a branch off a tree, that branch is "sexed," or "cut off." It is meant to be one with and united to that trunk of the tree, but now it is not – it is cut off.

To be born into this world is a similar phenomenon. We are created in the image of God, who is One and is able to hold both maleness and femaleness together. We, however, though born in God's image, cannot. Most of us, by God's design, are born either male or female, and that creates tension, a longing for wholeness, consummation, completeness, a dynamic energy that we call "Eros." That energy is also a divine energy, a divine fire within. In that sense, spirituality could also be defined as what we do with that divine inner fire.

Commenting on that divine fire, Richard Rohr would say, "Thus all healthy spirituality will always have a truly 'sexual' character to it, a desire for re-union. Religion is always, in one sense or another, about *making one out of two!*"[21]

Before going further, we need to be clear on three different aspects of human sexuality. There is a difference between human sexuality (gender – maleness or femaleness), genital sex (sexual intercourse) and love (*agape* or deep caring and intimate sharing). Many of our problems as human beings living out our daily lives come especially from a confusion of genital sex with love, as well as from an ignorance of the dynamics of our human sexuality.

We are physical, intellectual, emotional, relational and, especially, sexual beings. In all of us, there is a profound tension at the centre of our lives, a burning in the heart, a deep longing, a holy longing – an Eros.

For Ron Rolheiser, the tragedy is that so many persons, full of feelings and gifts and bursting with life, see this drive as something that is essentially irreligious, as something that sets them against what is spiritual. Nothing could be further from the truth. Our erotic impulses are God's lure in us. We experience them precisely as "spirit," as that which makes us more than mere animals. They are our spirit. This Eros is the basis of the spiritual life. It is in this sense that spirituality is an *erotic urge*. What we do with that Eros inside of us, whether heroic or pathetic, is our choice, but it *is* our spiritual life.

This spirit makes it impossible for us to be static. We must move outside of ourselves. This movement outward is experienced as a double tension (an inner hunger plus an attractive outside person or object that draws us outward). This tension is either beneficial for us or destructive for us. When it is beneficial, we experience a positive spiritual life; when it is destructive, we have a negative spiritual life.

Gerald May once again provides some key insights into this dynamism of our human sexuality: "In its fullest sense, then, sexuality is nothing other than creative spirit: basic energy directed towards the enrichment and expansion of life. All endeavours that point towards greater depth and breadth of life can be said to be sexual. In this light spiritual searching, from its outset, could be called a sexual undertaking."[22]

Within the limits of this illustration, and at the risk of being judgmental, I think it is probable that well-known personalities such as Elvis Presley, Janis Joplin, Amy Winehouse, Michael Jackson, Philip Seymour Hoffman and Robin Williams could be seen as having had a somewhat negative spiritual life. The case of Williams may be mitigated (or complicated) by the reality of co-occurring disorders that Hazelden, in its Internet column entitled *Behavioural Health Evolution*, defines as "persons having substance abuse disorders as well as mental health disorders." All died young for similar reasons (Joplin and Winehouse were only 27).

Physically, perhaps they pushed themselves too hard and did not take adequate care of themselves. Mentally, they were intelligent, but perhaps ignored the ramifications of some of the knowledge they carried that could have helped them walk in greater balance. In regards to emotional health, one wonders how well they were able to identify, name and share their emotions rather than act out of their especially painful emotions. In terms of relationships, I wonder how well they were able to enter into intimate, committed relationships with God and with others, and how aware they were of their own inner reality. Perhaps they also tended to misunderstand or were unable to handle the power of that "Eros," that divine fire within them. As Janis Joplin is reputed to have said, "I go out on stage and make love to two thousand people, and then I am supposed to sleep alone?" In the end, I wonder whether they are no longer with us because they lacked the ability to live positively that tension of their human incompleteness.

On the other hand, within this same way of looking at spirituality, I believe one can present a person such as Mother Teresa of Calcutta as one who had a positive spiritual life. A petite elderly celibate woman dressed simply in the distinctive white and blue sari of the religious order she founded, she had a tremendous Eros or inner divine fire. Energized by this powerful personal drive and love for herself, for God, for others and especially for the poor, she picked up the destitute and dying off the streets of Calcutta, gave them loving care and allowed them to die with dignity.

In a way that baffled yet impressed many, this diminutive, simple nun exerted a powerful influence over the rich and the powerful of this world, so much so that she was awarded the coveted Nobel Peace Prize. Her legacy, attested to by the tremendous outpouring of affection, respect and love from millions at the time of her exceptional state funeral in India, will live on for decades to come, because, I believe, she lived a very positive spiritual life.

An enigmatic figure placed somewhere in between the previous, more extreme examples of spiritual life is the late Diana, Princess of Wales. She also died young, like Joplin and Winehouse, and she shared many of the characteristics of a negative spiritual life (a broken relationship and flamboyant lifestyle towards the end, etc.). However, Diana was also in many ways akin to Mother Teresa. Diana showed concern for the disadvantaged, as well as personal commitment in acting on their behalf. Had she lived longer, she might have been able to develop that altruistic, compassionate side that she displayed at times, and might have had, in the end, a more positive spiritual life and legacy of her own.

Perhaps it was this very human, unfulfilled potential that allowed millions of people to identify with Diana and that touched their lives and hearts and underlay the amazing outpouring of grief and affection when she died so tragically and prematurely. It was as if death had cheated this fragile, suffering, yet beautiful and promising young woman of the opportunity to realize the spiritual journey she had begun.

The above examples are intended to help us grasp this spirituality of human incompleteness that I believe aids an understanding of the underlying dynamics of addiction and recovery. Key to this understanding is the feeling of "longing" or "incompleteness" that is part and parcel of being human. The tendency to misunderstand that longing as something negative, and the subsequent unfortunate attempts to medicate the pain of being human with something physical like alcohol or drugs, rather than to see this longing as a way to grow and to live a more fully human life, is, I believe, a root cause of addictive behaviour. The way that this "longing" combines with the dynamic of "loneliness" to lead people into addiction will be more fully explained in the section on "The Journey into Addiction."

In the spirit of Step Three (God as we understand God), I would like to close this section with one final thought based on the image that was used in *Illustration 08*. Letting the lines move into the centre of Eros, and thus completing the cross, signifies not repressing, ignoring or denying our sexuality, but rather letting God into it, finding God there, letting it be the door to the divine energy within us as a way of accepting our sexuality.

Now that we have considered a spirituality of wellness, let us explore the opposite of this wellness, the journey into addiction.

Suggested Activity

Part Two invites us to name and claim our own spirituality. As you look back upon the significant events of your life from the exercise in Part One, try to identify the definition that best describes the spirituality that has grounded you during those times you highlighted in your journal. Try also to identify the spirituality that has challenged you to new life. Has that spirituality changed over the years, and if so, how?

QUESTIONS FOR REFLECTION

1. Be present to three revealing questions: Who am I? Where am I from? Where am I going? If you are able to answer these questions for yourself, this will give a more profound insight into your own personal spiritual journey.
2. In what ways has your spiritual life been a "journey" versus a "hermitage"?
3. Which definition of spiritual life has been most life-giving for you?

PART THREE:
The Journey into Addiction

Having delved into the awesome reality of being fully human in Part One, and having grounded ourselves in various understandings of spirituality in Part Two, we are now ready to explore in greater detail the mystery of human suffering and the journey into addiction.

I believe that each of us can look back over our own unique participation in this pain of being human to a particular "Original Wound" or "Core Grief" that marked the beginning of our own suffering. The Big Book puts it this way: "Our liquor was but a symptom. So we had to get down to causes and conditions."[23] That original wound or core grief sets up certain patterns of reactions and behaviours that begin to characterize our lives and ultimately to lead many of us into addiction.

Before setting out and retracing that path to addiction, however, it would be helpful to grasp some underlying dynamics of the addictive process. Let us look first at the dynamics of the Dysfunctional Wheel.

The Dysfunctional Wheel of Unmet Needs

For the purpose of this section, I use the term "dysfunctional" to differentiate from functional. Every person or family has some level of dysfunction, as no person or family is perfect. This is not meant to be pejorative but rather descriptive. As the Big Book puts it, "A doctor said to us, 'Years of living with an alcoholic is almost sure to make any wife or child neurotic. The entire family is, to some extent, ill.'"[24]

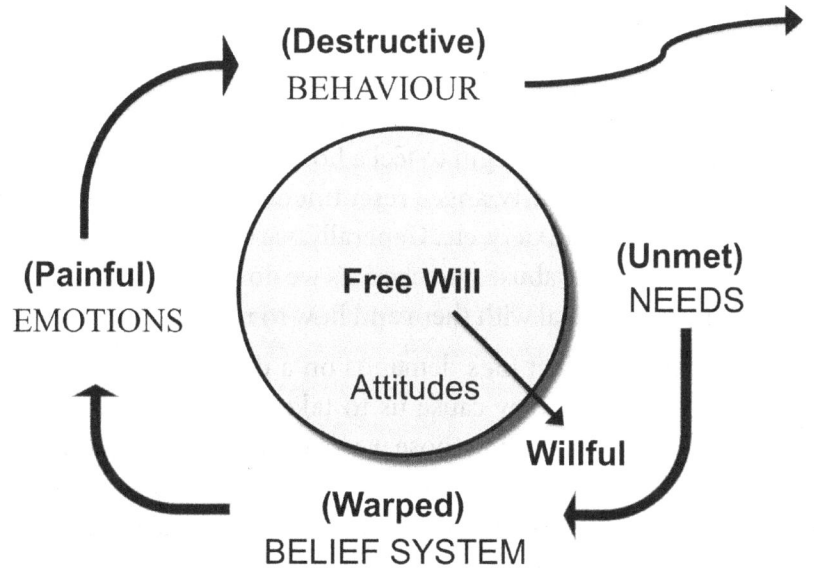

Illustration 09

Like the Awareness Wheel and the Wellness Wheel in Part One, this now becomes the Dysfunctional Wheel in Part Three. At the outset, the reality of our original wound or core grief can be summed up by the term "unmet needs." When our need to be loved, to belong and to be valued is not met, our belief system is assaulted. In many cases, we respond by believing we are not loved and we are actually unlovable. This results in that "stinking thinking" that is referred to in the program of A.A. as the following: "Selfishness – self-centeredness! That, we think, is the root of our troubles. Driven by a hundred forms of fear, self-delusion, self-seeking, and self-pity, we step on the toes of our fellows and they retaliate."[25]

Tempered and tempted with this belief of being unloved, our thoughts gravitate to negativity. Our reality reflects a negative outlook. Our interpretation of that reality will also be negative. Instead of seeing the glass as half full, we will consistently see it as half empty. Our beliefs will tend to be negative, and the judgments we make will take on a sour note.

Our decisions will become hurtful and harmful, based on the painful memories we hold. Our understanding, our conscience, our intuition and our imagination will all be impacted by a shadowy negativity that will infect not only our relationships with others, but also our view of ourselves and all that we do.

Our negative thinking or warped belief system has a direct impact upon our emotions. We begin to feel a host of unpleasant or painful feelings, such as insecurity, anger, resentment, confusion, loneliness, abandonment, fear, anxiety, etc. Generally, we will repress these feelings and emotionally abuse ourselves, as we do not know what to do with them, how to deal with them and how to rid ourselves of them.

Attempting to meet life's demands on a day-to-day basis when we are dysfunctional may cause us to take out our frustration on those closest to us, including those we love. The level of dysfunction is directly related to the frustration experienced, often escalating to violence, as we have seen earlier, and transmitting the pain that we don't transform.

A woman in a northern community who was carrying a heavy inner burden serves as an example. One day, she emerged from a store to see two women chatting close by. In her usual dysfunctional way, operating out of a lifetime of unmet needs, she immediately judged that they were talking about her. She angrily threw her purchases into her vehicle, revved up the motor, drove right up to them, slammed on the brakes, rolled down the window, swore at them and drove off.

Though saddened by her story, I was grateful for her courage to share her experience as an example of how unmet needs created a warped belief system that filled her with painful emotions, which in turn led her to act out with destructive behaviour.

The Unwritten Rules

Another background reality that sets us up for addiction is the presence of "Unwritten rules." These rules are defence mechanisms that we unconsciously internalize as we grow up trying to survive in our more or less dysfunctional families. These rules, in their simplest form, are

1. Don't talk
2. Don't trust
3. Don't feel

The issue of family loyalty is a source of these rules. The first rule children learn very early is not to talk to anyone about family matters. They learn to pretend that everything is okay, or they simply cannot find the words to articulate the complex reality of the family dynamics they are experiencing. They will make excuses and cover up for the addicted behaviour of the parent(s) or guardian.

A second rule that children learn quickly is not to trust. They become very distrustful of adults, including those who are trying to help them. This presents quite a challenge to caregivers who try to learn what is really happening in a family.

When children learn not to talk and not to trust, it is natural they cap that process by learning not to feel. Children are told, "You shouldn't feel like that" or "Don't cry. Everything is okay," when everything to them is obviously not okay, and they need to cry. As mentioned earlier, these are things my mother used to say when I was growing up. While I don't blame her, I realized years later that to heal I had to admit and face the legacy of codependency that she handed on to me, that ever-present tendency to please people and to minimize the painful reality I experienced. I was able to do this with the help of someone who first pointed out to me the need to focus on that source of hurt from my mother, as well as the more obvious hurt from my workaholic father.

The Survival Roles

Another underlying dynamic operative within any dysfunctional family where there is much unarticulated personal pain is the drive to survive. To accomplish this survival goal, children will adopt certain coping mechanisms or survival skills. Briefly, I want to highlight six such roles, all somewhat flexible and interchangeable.

The two basic roles in a dysfunctional family are the *Addict (Controller)* and the *Co-Addict (Co-dependent Enabler spouse/partner)*. The addict is basically in control of the family. Everything revolves around the addict. The spouse of the addict most often spends a lot of time and energy coping with the addict, either trying to control the addict or being controlled by the addict. The interaction between these two sets up the rest of the family to adopt the following roles for survival that I have observed in some families:

1. The Family Hero

This tends to be the eldest child, also known as the Responsible One. The Family Hero takes on the responsibility of raising the younger siblings, as the addicted parents are unable to give their children the attention they need. Usually, the parents are too wrapped up in their own dysfunction to notice that anything is wrong. And if they are aware, they are incapable of effecting a change, or they simply avoid the issue, hoping it will resolve itself.

The Hero willingly takes on this role, because it is a way of receiving some attention and affirmation, as well as arriving at a certain identity. Family Heroes are liked and admired, because they are usually high achievers and highly competent.

The down side is that they carry the guilt of the family. They usually find themselves cheated out of their childhood, having no time to play or to be a child, and they eventually run the risk of rebelling when this role no longer works for them. They often end up becoming very resentful of their parents and of life in general. They will tend to conform to the status quo, seeking a false wholeness in process addiction such as codependency, sexual activity or workaholism. Years later, these children usually have to deal with deep resentment over a lost childhood.

One Family Hero comes to mind immediately. The family was composed of the mother, who was a single parent, and eight children from four different fathers, none of whom were around. The mother was addicted to drugs, and when not absent from the home, she was high or stoned on substances.

The eldest daughter, at the age of 13, took on the mothering role, cooking, cleaning, dressing the youngest and watching over the children as they played, but rarely entering into the games herself.

A social worker would spend time with the family, playing with them. She remarked to me that the oldest girl didn't know how to play. It became obvious to the social worker that this girl felt more comfortable being a mother to her siblings than a playmate. I suspected that she would someday resent the loss of her childhood and the imposition of such responsibility, and sure enough, she eventually rebelled and became an unwed mother herself at the age of 16.

2. The Scapegoat

The Scapegoat, often the second-eldest child, is the one who sees the stability and responsibility of the older sibling, and, whether out of anger or jealousy, takes another path of acting out, rebelling, engaging in destructive behaviour and dabbling with substance abuse. The Scapegoat doesn't conform, is considered the "black sheep" of the family, and is often blamed for much of the family's troubles.

Surprisingly, this role is considered by experts to be the healthiest role. It is the Scapegoat who is most likely to get help for the family by revealing the family dysfunction and the painful family secrets, whereas all the other roles mask or cover that malaise.

I think here of another family in which a child who felt unwanted by her mother as well as abandoned by her father stabbed her younger sister in the head with a fork one day. What alarmed me was that this action was not seen as anything unusual by that particular family. She was the one who got into the most trouble at school and who found it difficult to relate with other children. She was also the one most blamed for the unrest at home, a true Scapegoat.

3. The Lost Child

Another role is that of the Lost or Withdrawn Child. In a dysfunctional family, this child will unconsciously pick up the message and the feeling of not being valued or wanted. The way this child copes with the pain of the dysfunction in the family is to escape and to avoid reality. They will be very quiet and well behaved, and will rarely act out. They repress and stuff their emotions. Unfortunately, this behaviour is often misinterpreted as "being good" and "angelic," leading others to think that everything is all right.

For the most part, the Lost Child will function reasonably well in school and later on in society, but no one ever gets to know them personally. They observe life, rather than participate in it. They also store up their emotions, rather than deal with them. The child caught in this role may well explode someday into inexplicable rage, for example, walking into a school and going on a shooting rampage. They are often the ones who "transmit the pain they do not transform," as we learned earlier. Fortunate are they when an adult can recognize this "perfect exterior" for what it is and draw out the bottled up emotions before they erupt in a destructive manner.

As a 13-year-old, I witnessed the painful reality of a Lost Child when visiting a certain family. I remember coming around the corner of a building and seeing the 14-year-old son, ordinarily quiet and well-behaved, grinding his teeth and growling at his father who was scolding him. I felt shock and fear, and at that young age could only turn and run away bewildered.

4. The Mascot

This role is also called the Comedian or Adapter, and often applies to a fourth child. They seem to learn from the other roles played by their older siblings, and often are able to cope in a somewhat healthier manner. These children seem to feel the pain of the family more markedly, but they cover that pain by trying to keep things light with humour or activity.

A friend shared with me that the Mascot was his role as he grew up. He remembers being the family bartender at the age of 11, serving everybody drinks when company came to make sure that everyone was happy. As he grew older, he used humour to help him cope, even to the point of sometimes inappropriate humour in his work and hurting people's feelings.

As more children come along, the roles tend to alternate or repeat. While different authors put forward other roles or different names for the same roles, the four described above will communicate the idea of their importance and how they portray life in a dysfunctional family. These roles work. They help children survive painful family situations.

As people heal from these roles, they find that the skills learned can become valuable assets for them later on in life. One such person is Dr. Maggie Hodgson, who was director of Training, Research and Health Promotion at the Nechi Institute in St. Albert, Alberta, for many years. She attributes her success to the survival skills she learned as a child in a dysfunctional family. Quite often, survivors become counsellors and caregivers, and find they are able to help others more effectively because they understand other survivors and know how to relate to them.

Some families I have worked with fit the pattern of these roles exactly, while others vary greatly. In general, knowing this pattern helps a caregiver understand the dynamics within a family. At the same time, these roles are not cast in stone and are susceptible to change. When being a Mascot no longer worked for my friend, he tried hard to be a Hero. When that did not work either, he rebelled, became a Scapegoat and starting acting out. He lost 10 percent on his academic average, failed an exam for the first time ever, missed out on a scholarship and graduated a very angry young man.

These survival roles incarcerate children in an invisible prison, and often leave them unable to communicate their inner painful reality. Needless to say, I have a deep respect for the impact these survival roles have on the lives of children in dysfunctional families.

What underlies these survival roles are defence mechanisms or coping skills. A defence mechanism is usually an unconscious method for reducing anxiety and restoring self-esteem. Defence mechanisms are necessary for survival, but become problematic when they dominate behaviour and prevent resolution of issues, healing and growth later in life. People need to move beyond these defence mechanisms, or they will stunt their personal development. One way of putting this is that we cannot live the second half of life with the same rules by which we lived the first half.

The Three Options

Psychologists generally offer two options whenever danger confronts us, options we are likely familiar with: *fight* or *flight*. However, a friend who had been terribly sexually abused by her father taught me a third option: *freeze*. She told me that whenever her father came in "tipsy," she would hold her breath, stay motionless and try to make herself invisible. To see these three options in a clearer light, I have put them into the following format:

Fight – (Fury)
Flight – (Fear)
Freeze – (Fear)

These are instinctive survival techniques used by both animals and humans. They are normal and understandable. If we are anger-based persons (Fury), we will automatically react to hurt by *fighting back* in anger, taking revenge, getting even, tit for tat. This reaction occurs so often, it almost appears normal. Even the Old Testament teaching of "an eye for an eye and a tooth for a tooth" (Leviticus 24:17), although intended to limit violence by putting boundaries around reactions to violence, has been quoted as justification for all-out retribution. Having been so grossly misunderstood, it is a poor and inadequate response to hurt.

On the other hand, with a fear-motivated personality, one would normally react to hurt by *fleeing or running away*. These people will run away out of fear; they disassociate themselves from the turmoil; they remove themselves as best they can from the equation.

Some ways of fleeing may be indulging in alcohol or drugs or some other addictive activity, such as sex, gambling, excessive sports, work, etc., even "the silent treatment" – anything that will numb our pain or provide us with an excuse not to deal with a difficult issue or individual in our lives.

The response of the freeze personality comes from a reaction to abuse and trauma. Someone who has been the subject of trauma in one's life may be filled with terror and not know how to protect themselves except by *freezing*, trying to become invisible, trying not to be seen or heard. The danger here is that this may also freeze and numb their emotions so that they become wooden. This increases the risk of developing physical symptoms of illness that flow out of suppressed emotions.

A woman I was counselling shared with me that she forgot to tell her father when her son died. Shocked, I asked how she felt about this. When she replied that she felt nothing, I suggested to her that perhaps she felt numb, like a piece of wood. She identified with that immediately as a flash of self-awareness lit up her darkness and took her a step closer to healing. She had suppressed her emotions for so long, emotions that were unvalidated, undifferentiated and unnamed, that they had literally frozen and had morphed into numbness. This is similar to the dull grey that results when one mixes many colours of paint. This grey, I pointed out to her, was also an emotion, albeit the frozen emotion of numbness.

While these three options are useful and help us survive, they will eventually leave us unsatisfied and stuck if we do not learn to live life rather than merely to survive it. Something beyond these options has to happen to move us onward on our healing journey. A fourth, much healthier option will be presented in the chapter on our healing journey.

The Three Temptations

Members in the program sometimes refer to an obsession with money, fame and power as the cause of their troubles. The temptation to abuse these can be powerful. As mentioned in Part One, they connect with the three temptations that Jesus faced in the desert. To the extent that our faith in God who loves us is battered and bruised, the power and pull of these temptations grows. I prefer to label them the three Ps: possessions, prestige and power.

Father Thomas Keating, promoter of the Centering Prayer movement, describes the same reality: "The diseased roots of our inner tree are the excessive energy that we put into finding happiness through the gratification of unlimited and unreal demands for the symbols in the culture of safety/security, affection/esteem/approval and power/control."[26]

The first temptation, *possessions*, is very logical. Fundamentally, as human beings we are made for relationships. We either relate to someone or to some "thing." Because of the hurt in our lives, we lose our faith in the spiritual, such as love, and place our trust in something physical, such as alcohol, drugs, money, food, clothes or cars that we can possess, or in some process activity such as music, gambling and genital sex, in which we can find some fleeting pleasure.

The second temptation, *prestige*, is more complex and demands a closer look to help us understand this temptation. Let's look at this for our purpose now in dealing with this temptation. As we suffer from a lack of love in our lives, our human security is chipped away and is replaced by insecurity. Instead of dealing with the pain caused by that insecurity in positive and helpful ways, instinctively we attempt an antidote of self-aggrandizement and grandiosity. This gives us a false sense of security, because it has emerged from an attempt to compensate for a lack of love or security in our lives. Our need for security may also masquerade as a desire for prestige, because we want to look good to others and also to ourselves.

In order to accomplish this, it may well be that we demean others and speak about their shortcomings. Even more harmful, we may engage in gossip, a devastating social scourge in our society. In fact, gossip may have become the most common and prevalent societal addiction.

An example of the extent to which this need for prestige can drive human behaviour is the student who showed up at a high school and randomly shot students and a teacher before taking his own life. He left behind a suicide note claiming that this act would make him famous. That is a sick need for recognition, particularly because it is dependent upon harm done to innocent others.

The third temptation, in a less dramatic fashion, is *power*. Power is seductive and exhilarating. I believe that sexual abuse of innocent children is not so much a matter of pleasure as it is a sick need for power over another human being. Power over another person provides a "rush" that is heady and thrilling. Murder is probably the ultimate such "rush." The sick need for control in relationships is related to this craving for power and the rush that power provides.

The biblical account of the temptations of Jesus in the desert (Matthew 4:1-11) provides an enlightening affirmation for those in the program who struggle with money, fame and power. To say the least, the inspired writers of the Bible were good psychologists, preceding the program by millennia but articulating and presenting the same wisdom.

The first temptation Jesus faced was to turn stones into bread (possessions). The second temptation that the devil taunted Jesus with was to throw himself down from the Temple and force the angels to come and rescue him (prestige). The third temptation was to bow down and worship Satan, and he would be given all the kingdoms of the world (power). In this last temptation especially, one sees how addiction is ultimately the worship of a false god.

Here we are reminded of Dlugos' insight described in Part One on Human Be-ing about the two kinds of sin: to be more than human and to be less than human.

That was the basic temptation that Jesus faced in the desert. He was tempted to be more than human (to rise above pain and suffering) and to be less than human (to let himself slide into dissipation). The response of Jesus to these three temptations at his weakest, most vulnerable moment was a total rejection of these false gods and an unqualified, total trust in his loving relationship with the Father.

The evil one was mocking him with these temptations: how can you be the Son of God if you are poor, a nobody, and have no power? The response of Jesus was based on his faith in the Father's love: he could be the Son of God without these things. It was like he was saying he would take the steps down from the tower of the Temple like everyone else. He chose to remain fully human, to stay with the ordinary rather than escape into the extraordinary. He refused the temptations to use his divine power in a selfish way.

Walk a New Path

I have come to appreciate Jesus as the one who totally and completely rejected slavery in his life, the one who was totally free from any addiction. We, however, have to contend with addiction that is the hallmark of our modern society. With all of the above as background, let us now turn our attention to our struggle with addiction, and more specifically, to the all-too-common journey into addiction.

The Journey into Addiction

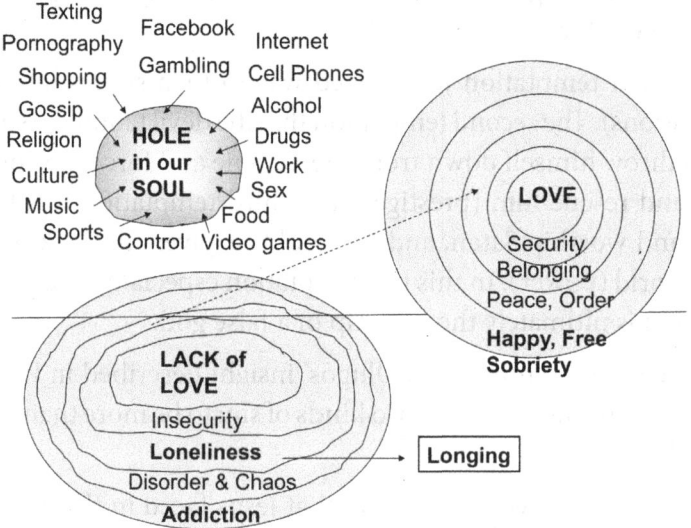

Illustration 10

Have you ever seen inside a softball? The softballs that I used to play with as a youngster were made up of a leather covering over string wound around a core of India rubber that gave the ball its bounce. A ball with no bounce is taken out of the game. It has lost its ability to function as a ball and loses its value for the game.

Let the Twelve Steps give you the "bounce," the love you need to accept and to live the challenge of the game of life.

A softball is destined to be hit by a bat for the sake of the game. So also we human beings are destined to encounter problems for the sake of life. We are like that ball. We all have a covering. Some coverings are soft and healthy. Others are thick, crusty with denial, defence mechanisms, blame and escapism, or are thin, easily bruised and broken. Just below the surface, some are full of positive experiences. Others are all wound up with past hurts. For all of us, at our centre is a core that is love or a lack of love.

It is this core of love, or lack of love, that makes all the difference in the game of life. Many of us, because of dysfunctional backgrounds and a lack of love, spend our energy trying to avoid pain, suffering and more hurt. We desperately skirt issues, problems and difficulties only to find that there is really no healthy way around them. We must stop, face them and name them sooner or later to play the game of life.

The illustration provided for this section depicts two balls. For the sake of this diagram, envisage them as two beach balls floating in the water: one floating on top, one about to sink.

These two balls symbolize two lives: one functional and based on love, the other dysfunctional and based on the unfortunate experience of a lack of love.

The Love Pattern

Let's examine the functional "ball" or "love pattern" first. Five attributes stand out in causing this ball to float.

- Love

The person symbolized by this ball grows up in a family where there is a lot of love, both perceived and actual. Emotional needs are met and there is lots of expressed sincere affection, trust, acceptance and open communication.

Vanier describes this positive reality in his own candid way:

A child, born into a deeply united family, discovers his own value through the loving presence of his parents. He gains confidence in himself, discovering that he is a unique human being, infinitely precious, because his parents treated him that way. He knows that everything he does, good or bad, touches the heart of his mother. If he does something good, she is happy and laughs; if he does something bad, she is unhappy. Whatever he does provokes profound emotion in the hearts of those who love him. He is not treated as an indifferent human being.[27]

- Security

This beloved individual will early in life show lots of "bounce," which leads to a sense of security, well-being and self-esteem. Children who know they are loved and feel secure will have a good sense of identity, purpose and direction. These qualities will continue to grow, enabling them to meet life's challenges.

- Belonging

A second characteristic of a healthy, functional person is a feeling of belonging. Children who know they are loved and feel secure within themselves know they belong. Already, two of their deepest human needs, to be loved and to belong, are being met. These individuals manifest this by their enjoyment of their families and their home life. They are comfortable, and actually like being at home.

One summer, a youth volunteer came to our community from another province. He had come from a dysfunctional family background, and he had more problems than those he had come to help. He was amazed at one close-knit family and how the members of that family actually looked forward to coming home from school and university just to be together and enjoy each other's company with a lot of singing, horseplay and laughter. He had rarely witnessed this kind of close family life in the city. This experience challenged him to take some steps to improve his relationship with his own family.

- Peace and Order

When someone feels that they belong, they experience a sense of peace and order. The lives of children in this kind of family usually exhibit a marked absence of crisis. There is normality and a healthy predictability about life. Things seem to fall into place. These children do well in school, become involved in activities, perhaps get jobs on the side, make friends easily enough and basically go about life developing their hobbies, skills and talents in that process of self-actualization that the renowned psychologist Maslow writes about.

- Happy, Free Sobriety

The result of this love pattern is a person and, by extension, a family that is basically happy and free of addiction. Problems will come to this person and this family, but they will have the bounce and the love they need to handle these problems in a functional and healthy way. In fact, these very problems will become a means of growth for them. Instead of being overwhelmed and devastated by the presence of problems, they will be able to meet each problem as a challenge to grow, to become stronger and to improve themselves.

For them, life is not a problem to be solved, but a mystery to be lived. If a crisis or insult or problem comes their way, they are like beach balls buoyed up by the love and pleasant emotions inside the cover. When pushed down, they just bounce up somewhere else, forgive and carry on.

It's always a joy and a privilege to relate to such persons and families. I remember meeting such a family one day and being greeted by the six-year-old daughter, who asked me if I had a button like the one she was wearing. When I answered "no," she took hers off and, without a moment's hesitation, said, "Here, I'll give you mine."

That child knew she was loved. She was secure and able to give. She belonged, was at peace and was a happy, free child who I knew was emotionally equipped to handle whatever would come her way in life.

In fact, as an adult she was able to cope with a serious, life-threatening illness with patience, humour and strong faith. Though that illness eventually claimed her life, she faced death with an impressive, almost majestic calm, presence of mind, loving last words with her family and peaceful acceptance of that final passage of her life.

The Lack of Love Pattern

Turning now to the ball without bounce, we see that the "Lack of Love Pattern" is just the opposite of the "Love Pattern." The core is weak through a lack of love, for whatever reason. At the outset of this section, I want to point out that I have learned to use the term "lack of love" rather than "unloved," because no one is totally unloved – all of us are loved by others in some way. However, the lack of love that we experience becomes our original wound and the core grief that forms the basis of this painful pattern in our lives.

- Lack of Love

In this pattern, love may not be coming to us in the way that we need to receive it at a particular time in our lives. For example, the way my workaholic father chose to express his love for us was to work harder to provide for our material needs, when all I wanted from him was to spend time together, to go fishing or hunting, something we never did.

Sometimes the love is present, but unavailable, as in the case of parents who are home, but are aloof, distant, uncommunicative, showing little affection. This can be an even greater hurt than an alcoholic parent who may be abusive but at least recognizes the presence of the other. The parents of a participant in a particular therapy group were not obviously addicted to anything, but they were emotionally distant from her. She was the angriest of all the participants, and nearly destroyed the materials she had been given to express her anger.

A more obvious display of a lack of love is rejection, dislike or addiction that removes the adult from the home, harms relationships and renders home life impossible. Rigid families and overly religious families can also manifest a lack of love. Of course, broken families have a devastating effect on children. A young person's paramount fear is abandonment. The loss of their greatest source of security, parents who love each other, gives rise to great fear. Those who experience this fear need special care and attention.

Sometimes, a child will perceive a lack of love within circumstances over which neither the child nor the family have any control, such as illness or death. The consequences, however, are just as present and real as if the situation had been intentional. This is key to a deeper understanding of the influences in a child's life.

Jean Vanier describes this negative reality in these words: "He may feel rejected. He may have a deep feeling of solitude ... loneliness. And from this anguish can be born many things ... For when I am in this state of anguish I try to escape it by refusing life and reality. I risk falling into a serious psychosis. I refuse reality because reality means hatred and abandonment."[28]

A more extreme case of lack of love is that of abuse – physical, verbal, mental, emotional or sexual. As we have seen, the deepest wound comes from sexual abuse. The term for that abuse, or any extreme form of abuse, is trauma, which necessitates an in-depth healing process. Many books and workshops exist on this topic alone. This lack of love breaks the spirit, warps the minds and bruises the emotions of young children, often rendering them emotionally dysfunctional. Such dysfunction is expressed especially by human insecurity, to which we turn our attention now.

- Human Insecurity

The primary characteristic that flows from this lack of love, whatever form it takes, is human insecurity. One of our deepest human needs, to be loved, is violated or denied. We become emotionally insecure, especially because of the "mixed messages" often found in alcoholic homes. When a child knows she or he is loved, all is well. On the other hand, when a child knows that a step-parent dislikes him or her, then they will find someone else who can love them, perhaps a grandparent or uncle or aunt.

If, however, a child is praised and affirmed for a certain behaviour one day and is punished and beaten for the same behaviour the next day because of an alcoholic parent's irrational mood swings, then the child becomes confused. Is he or she loved or not? While the child hopes that she is loved, she fears that she is not. The child doesn't know, and may become emotionally insecure, distrustful and fearful. This insecurity can actually be more devastating and harder to deal with than blatant abuse.

- Loneliness

Insecurity is a terrible feeling, which leads quickly to the next characteristic, an equally terrible loneliness and feeling of abandonment, as well as lack of self-worth or self-esteem. A child doesn't feel like he or she belongs. There emerges a deep loneliness, which is neither solitude nor the ability to be alone with oneself in a healthy way. This loneliness grips the heart and affects the spirit. It is usually accompanied by strong feelings of anger, resentment, jealousy and confusion, not to mention sadness, emptiness and self-pity.

These raw, painful emotions get all jumbled up in an inchoate mess within a child's heart, and they create a feeling like a "hole in our soul" so that the spirit begins to weep. Children begin to wear masks, enter into denial, justify those they love, blame themselves and, in essence, lose their True Self and begin to develop a false self.

We saw in Part Two how, at the core of our human be-ing, we already have an innate sense of *longing*, of incompleteness, a restlessness that must be handled positively. This longing or desire for wholeness is integral to being born into this world. Add deep *loneliness* and *woundedness* from the lack of love to this intricate and complex longing, and the result is a vulnerability that is overwhelming, devastating and a breeding ground for addiction.

- Chaos and Disorder

The next stage is chaos, disorder or destructive behaviour. Without understanding what is going on, and unable to grasp or articulate this subconscious inner process, a child will "act out" to express in some fashion what he or she is experiencing. The child acts out to cope and survive by expressing pent-up emotions, or, alternatively, acts out as a cry for help. It's like a volcano. Everything seems normal on the outside, but inside, very intense emotions have been building up for a long, long time, and now they start erupting, demanding expression.

It is here that children will adopt one or the other survival role. Family Heroes become caretakers. Scapegoats will get into all kinds of trouble or run away. Lost children will detach and escape into dream worlds. Mascots will try to keep everything light.

Individuals in this stage of crisis will desperately begin trying to fill that vacuum at the centre of their being, the "hole in their soul." Their belief in a loving God is almost gone. They fall for the temptation to put their trust in physical, material things they can see and feel, or in events and actions that give them a semblance of security and a sense of identity, control and importance. They start fighting, swearing, stealing and disobeying. Then the substance abuse begins: glue and/or gas sniffing, alcohol and drugs. As they grow older, the stakes get higher: theft, alcohol, gang life and irresponsible sex enter the picture.

Almost anything or anyone can be used: food, gossip, sports, gambling, shopping, music, etc. All are attempts to medicate the pain within. Even religion, culture and work can be used to numb the pain. These last activities are especially difficult to deal with, because they look so good. Why would anyone want to question someone who behaves well, plays, prays, studies and works hard? But the bottom line remains – if any of these activities are abused and serve as a substitute for a healthy relationship with God, oneself and others, they become the roots of addiction.

This "soul pain" constantly demands to be addressed. Unfortunately, most people are ill equipped to deal with this hurt, and they turn to false gods of all kinds to medicate their pain. They act out of their emotions in all kinds of chaotic ways, instead of dealing with their emotions. This takes us to the final stage of this journey.

- Addiction

The last stage in the journey into addiction is, of course, addiction itself. The more our faith in the spiritual is shaken, the more often we respond by succumbing to the temptations of possessions, prestige and power. Sooner or later, as a result of medicating our pain instead of dealing with our issues, we find ourselves trapped in the prison of substance abuse (chemical addiction) or attached to some event or person that begins to consume and control us (process addiction).

Whatever false god we have chosen as the object of our need for relationships and as our way of coping with our hurt will turn around to entrap us in an addiction. Slowly, we become an alcoholic, a drug addict, a workaholic, a sex addict, a chronic gossiper, perhaps even a criminal. We are no longer free but enslaved, and no longer have any "bounce" to face our problems. Any difficulty in life simply serves as another reason to practise our addiction, whatever it is, to turn to our false gods and to drive ourselves into deeper misery and perhaps even to our own death. One day it dawned on me that when we lose our faith in God who loves us, we place our faith in false gods that don't love us, that will entrap and eventually destroy us.

Addiction is such a common and much-used word that there may be some danger that its meaning and impact may be taken for granted. Let us examine some definitions of addiction before exploring what has come to be my own working definition.

Some Definitions of Addiction

1. Addiction is obsessive-compulsive behaviour.

This is perhaps the most obvious and observable aspect of an addiction. Many who are in a relationship with an alcoholic cannot understand why the person cannot stop or at least control their excessive drinking, especially when their behaviour has such obvious painful and often catastrophic results.

The answer is that someone who suffers from obsessive-compulsive behaviour has a disease or illness. The obsessive aspect involves continually mentally dwelling on the addictive behaviour, while the compulsive aspect means that the person simply can't stop or rein in the behaviour, try as they might.

One woman who has a gambling addiction shared with me her weekly routine. By Thursday, she has finished scheming and planning for her weekend gambling excursion, including the money and transportation. By Friday, she is off to the casino. On Sunday evening, she returns home, remorseful, angry, guilt-ridden, ashamed and resolving to change her life. By Tuesday, life is settling down, the feelings of Sunday are gone, and she has a good day. By Wednesday, however, those other thoughts return – "I can play smarter; it's my turn to win; I didn't lose that much; I'll stop myself before I lose it all; I can get it all back." By Thursday, the cycle is complete and starts over again. Addiction is truly obsessive-compulsive behaviour.

2. Addiction is an attempt to avoid legitimate suffering.

This definition came to me from John Bradshaw in his writings and at a 1991 conference in Saskatoon. As mentioned above, there are some lessons in life that we learn only through pain and suffering. Many people are so wounded by life's hurts and so ill equipped to deal with them that they absolutely do not want to be hurt anymore. They will do anything they can to avoid suffering and pain. They do not understand that the only way through the pain is through the pain.

These wounded and fragile individuals believe the only way to insulate themselves from pain and suffering or to deal with hurt is to medicate themselves with excessive alcohol or drugs or to overindulge in any kind of activity that distracts or detracts from the pain. For many people, addiction is an attempt to avoid legitimate suffering.

Here is how John Bradshaw puts it: "Our addictions and compulsivities are our mood-alterers. They are what we develop when we numb out. They are our ways of being alive and our ways of managing our feelings." He continues, "Addiction has become our national lifestyle (or rather death style). It is a death style based on the relinquishment of the self as a worthwhile being to a self who must achieve and perform or use something outside of self in order to be loveable and happy. Addictions are pain-killing substitutes for legitimate suffering. To legitimately suffer we have to feel as bad as we feel." In his comments on the compulsive family in general, Bradshaw concludes, "As far as I'm concerned, all addictions are ways to avoid unacceptable feelings. That avoidance leads to life-damaging consequences."[29]

3. Addiction is an illusion and a lie.

This definition came from a client at a rehabilitation centre where I was giving a workshop. The more I thought about it, the more I realized and appreciated its simple truth. An addiction always seems so attractive and enticing, and appears so often as the solution to one's problems, when in truth it is just the opposite – an illusion and a lie. I know a woman who had an accident while driving when she was impaired. She told a friend that she felt misunderstood by others, and that alcohol was not her problem; it was her solution for the other issues in her life. Anyone who thinks that alcohol is a "solution" to anything is living an illusion.

Once one has admitted or acknowledged an addiction, and is tempted to take that first drink or drug, or to engage in some risky activity that promises to provide solace, pleasure or illegitimate relief from personal pain, they need to be reminded that addiction is an illusion and a lie.

4. Addiction is a form of idolatry, worshipping a false god.

Fr. Jonathan ended up in a rehabilitation centre for clergy and religious after his burnout in ministry. There he was told by a fellow client that he was breaking the first of the Ten Commandments: "I am the Lord your God; you shall not have false gods before me."

A priest who had dedicated his life to ministry, Fr. Jonathan was shocked by this accusation. He initially resisted it, and resented his accuser. However, as he progressed in his treatment, he began to realize the truth in this statement. He indeed had been working himself into exhaustion slowly, progressively, out of a need to medicate the pain of unresolved family of origin and inner child issues. As long as he was busy ministering to others and appeared to be in control, he had no time to feel his own pain and deal with his inner emptiness.

Finally, Fr. Jonathan ended up crashing, spiritually bankrupt, with no desire or ability to pray or do anything. In treatment, he learned that his pace of life was literally killing him. He finally accepted the truth that he was worshipping the false god of work. He then began to make progress and to heal. While one would not normally think of work as a form of idolatry, when it becomes an addiction, it is capable of becoming a false god that can be worshipped.

Along this same line is the following definition of addiction from Ernest Kurtz and Katherine Ketcham:

Addiction represents the ultimate effort to control, the definitive demand for magic ... and the final failure of spirituality. Turning to the "magic" of chemicals signifies the desperate (and doomed) attempt to fill a spiritual void with a material reality, to make magic substitute for miracle. Addiction has been described as the belief that whenever there is "something wrong with me," it can be "fixed" by something outside of me. That false state generates even more drastic illusions. The search for the "quick fix" inevitably unfulfilled by drugs and unsated by material things, leaps next to spiritual realities and the search for an "instant spirituality," some sort of quick spiritual fix. It is no wonder, then, that locating "divinity in drugs" becomes a kind of spiritual death.[30]

Authors such as Bradshaw, Kurtz and Ketcham provide a deeper understanding of the situation in which Fr. Jonathan found himself. All of this simply underlines once again how cunning, baffling and powerful addiction is when it can entrap in its deadly grip even clergy and religious dedicated to serving God. Addiction respects no person and knows no limits. It can afflict the high or the lowly, the scholar or the student, the preacher or the penitent, the genius or the simple one.

A Working Definition of Addiction

The working definition of addiction that I have come up with for myself over the years, influenced by sources such as the World Health Organization, Craig Nakken and Dr. Durand F. Jacobs, is as follows:

Addiction is a pathological relationship with a mood altering substance, person or event that leads to life-damaging consequences, based on an abnormal physiologic arousal state (either hypertensive or hypotensive) and childhood experiences of trauma or lack of love that have produced a deep sense of personal inadequacy and rejection.[31]

According to Wikipedia, *pathological* means altered or caused by disease. Webster's dictionary describes it as being ill to a degree that is extreme, excessive or markedly abnormal. Addiction is a disease;

people who are ill need medical attention. The acceptance of addiction as an illness by the medical profession has been a major and invaluable breakthrough in terms of coping with addiction.

At the risk of taking some liberties with medical data, I would go even further to state that pathological means not just illness, but a death-dealing illness, an illness that kills. To my mind, a pathologist is one who seeks to discover the cause of a person's death. Though fear is not the best motive for discouraging people from entering into addictive behaviour, this knowledge alone should shake us up a bit, and perhaps prevent some from choosing the addictive path, a path that ultimately may lead to death.

An addiction is also a *relationship*, albeit a sick one. As human beings, we are made for relationships and have a deep human need to belong. Indeed, we need relationships just to sustain our humanity. However, because of the hurt in our past and our loss of faith, we no longer choose to maintain healthy, functional relationships with God, others or even ourselves. As a result, we enter into destructive relationships with substances like alcohol or drugs, with events such as sex or gambling, or with persons whom we either try to control or allow to control us, which is codependency.

Critical in the above definition is the term *mood altering*. Whatever or whomever we choose as the object of our attachment or relationship alters our mood, changes our feelings and makes us feel different. It medicates our pain, the pain that we don't understand, don't want and can't seem to control any other way. Very definitely, and sometimes very quickly, when we use or abuse, the immediate results are a euphoria or rush that becomes our be-all and end-all, our false god, the object of our time, money and energy.

Though I am not a chemically addicted person, I experienced some insight into the power of chemical addiction before undergoing knee surgery in a hospital. I had chosen a spinal block rather than undergoing anesthesia. I remember distinctly that sudden and extreme rush of giddiness, gladness, even euphoria when the chemical took effect. All was well with the world. It was like being in heaven, to the point of being scary. I remember thinking, "Wow, what a great feeling – why can't life always be like this?" Yet deep down, I knew that this was not real but artificial and temporary, the result of taking the chemical. It was, as defined earlier, an illusion and a lie. I was able to remind myself of that, which helped me stay grounded in reality. The rush, though, was very real, and I can see how vulnerable people could get addicted to such a powerful feeling of well-being, artificial as it is.

Jacob's Theory, the last part of the definition, posits two main character predispositions, *hypertensive* and *hypotensive*. A hypertensive personality is predisposed to being hyper and active, needing a lot of stimuli to have a sense of well-being. A hypotensive personality is predisposed to respond to life's situations in a subdued, more melancholy, quasi-depressed manner.

Jacob's research concludes that when either of these two predispositions is combined with some experience of trauma and/or lack of love leading to feelings of inadequacy or rejection, then a pathological attachment or addiction to some chemical, event or person is often the result. This insight links up with the temptation described earlier by Dlugos to be either more than human (hypertensive) or less than human (hypotensive). Addiction is about moving in either of those two directions rather than choosing to be just fully human.

Kinds of Addictions

It is important to keep in mind that there are two kinds of addictions: chemical addiction and process addiction. Chemical addiction includes addiction to alcohol, prescription drugs, street drugs, solvents, etc. Process addiction includes things such as shopping, gambling, sex, pornography, work, religion, culture, gossip, codependency, Internet, video games, and many more things too numerous to mention.

Addiction to work is what I learned and grew up with. I still have to contend with this within myself, having learned and absorbed it from my father. An example will illustrate.

When I was stationed in Beauval as a missionary Oblate priest, I needed to travel to Saskatoon, five hours away. My hometown of

North Battleford was on the way. This allowed me an opportunity to visit my parents, whom I had not seen for months. I called my mother to inform her that I would be coming for supper and asked her to tell Dad.

When I arrived at the farm, although supper was ready, there was no sign of my father. My mother said he was probably out in a field somewhere. We visited for an hour, then ate. On my way out, I decided to try to find my father. Sure enough, he was on the tractor cultivating a nearby field. I waited until he worked his way to the car, and I got on for a round. I asked my father why he had not come for supper, and he replied in French, "Je peux finir ce morceau ici ce soir si je continue." "I can finish this part tonight if I keep going."

I could hardly believe my ears. He had not seen me for months, and would not see me again for months; yet he *could not* stop working for even a couple of hours to visit with his son. That is compulsion. That is work addiction.

I felt angry, diminished, devalued, small, put down, worth less than the ground he was cultivating. Now I can understand the dynamics of this addiction, but at that time, it served only to drive the wedge between us even deeper. It dumped fuel on my self-righteous anger towards my father that I carried for years. Such is the devastation caused by work addiction.

Another process addiction that is surfacing more and more in society is religious addiction. I remember getting a call from a man who wanted me to come to his home for a session with his adult children. He said that we were going to listen to the young people for a change. This man had been an active alcoholic for over 20 years. Then he had a conversion experience, found Jesus and had been sober for about a dozen years. The problem was that he was always preaching to his family and others about Jesus, rather than working the steps or dealing with his issues.

When he invited me over and said that we were going to listen to the young people, I could not refuse. However, he began talking and preaching, which went on for half an hour. Finally, I interrupted him to remind him that he had promised we were going to listen to the young people, who so far had not said a word.

As respectfully as I could, I asserted that I would like to hear from his adult children. I then turned to his son and asked him how he felt about what was happening. He responded by intellectualizing something that he knew would be okay with his dad. I turned to the youngest daughter and asked her the same question. She responded in the same way.

Becoming desperate, I turned to the eldest daughter and asked her how she felt about what was transpiring in this session. She replied by saying that she thought her dad should stop preaching to the whole village and start listening to his family. I felt hope surge within and told her that this was a thought, not a feeling, but that I agreed with her completely. I then asked her again to share her feelings. As she began, her father actually physically leaned forward and waved his hands in front of her to stop her from sharing. I was shocked. The man who had invited me to come over so that we could both listen to his adult children was literally now blocking his oldest daughter from sharing her feelings about the way he had raised his family as a practising alcoholic.

I felt sad and discouraged. I left, realizing the futility of continuing the charade. As I drove away, it dawned on me that I had just witnessed a case of religious addiction. This man was escaping from his past and his pain into what looked like faith and religion, but was really only religiosity and the trappings of religion. I believe that this was religious addiction, behaviour that medicated his feelings and excused him from dealing with his issues.

The words of the Big Book came back to me: Addiction is "cunning, baffling and powerful."[32] I had just experienced it in one of its most deceptive forms, religious addiction. It is this reality that keeps people stuck and precludes any apology or making amends. It ultimately prevents those so addicted from ever being really free. They exist only in the illusion of it, and are truly to be pitied.

Although treating any addiction is a challenge, I think that process addictions pose a special obstacle. When recovering alcoholics attend an A.A. meeting, they do not take alcohol to the meeting. When recovering drug addicts attend a Narcotics Anonymous meeting, they do not bring drugs with them. When recovering codependents attend a CoDa meeting, however, they bring their codependency with them and risk practising their addiction right at the meeting itself. In a similar way, a workaholic cannot simply stop working. Process addiction is very much cunning, baffling and powerful. Certainly, anyone struggling with process addiction needs and deserves all the understanding and assistance they can get.

The Spiritual Cage

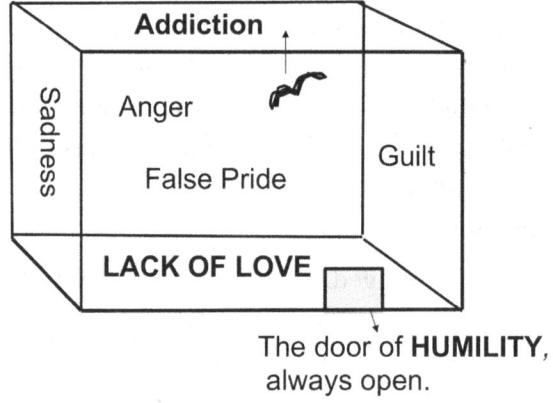

Illustration 11

A unique way of looking at the end result of the journey into addiction was taught to me by a sparrow. Seriously, a little bird gave me a deeper understanding of the addictive process. The story goes like this.

One Saturday evening, I was getting ready for the Sunday morning celebration in the old church in Beauval, when I noticed a sparrow flying around in the church. At first, I barely gave it a thought, and then I realized that the sparrow would be a distraction during the liturgy. I decided to get the sparrow out of the church, and quickly saw that I had a dilemma on my hands. This task would be easier said than done.

After a bit of thought, I decided to wait until dusk and to leave the door open with the porch light on. Surely the sparrow would fly towards the light and out the door on its own. Of course, this did not happen. Next, I decided to encourage the sparrow with a broom. It flew everywhere else except towards the door. Now the fight was on. I chased that elusive sparrow for the next 10 minutes. In the process, it tried to fly through every window, it landed on every statue and bounced off the ceiling; it flew everywhere but out that open door.

Finally, both of us exhausted, the sparrow landed on one of the iron rods overhead that connected the two walls of the church. It was puffing and unable to fly anymore. I stepped up on a pew and gently placed a finger behind the little sparrow's legs. It could do little else but climb backwards onto my finger, still puffing and petrified with fear. With the bird perched on my finger, I carefully stepped down off the pew and walked out the door, carrying the sparrow on my finger. I headed towards the rectory to show my "catch" to my brother, who was visiting me at the time, when suddenly it flew away, having got its wind back.

As I watched it disappear into the evening sky, a spiritual awareness dawned on me. That sparrow became a metaphor for me. The sparrow was caught in a building, unable to get out. All I wanted to do was help it, but there was a problem. The sparrow did not understand my motives, did not trust me, was afraid of me and tried to save itself, to no avail. Not until it exhausted itself and landed on the rod could it receive my help and be carried out of its dilemma.

Is that not all too often our own story? We are like a little bird, caught in a spiritual cage of our own making as a result of our hurt and loss of faith. The bottom of our cage is a lack of love or some kind of trauma. The cage is full of insecurity and loneliness as we build invisible walls around ourselves using our survival skills. The front wall is made up of false pride and stubbornness and a brave outward appearance as we deny that anything is wrong. The back wall is built with invisible bricks of anger and resentment that we repress until they explode. The side walls are sadness and self-pity, guilt and fear as we react to hurt, refuse to forgive, resist help and retreat into our wounded selves. Finally, the ceiling is an addiction. Whatever substance, event or person we choose to relate to in a pathological manner, as a futile attempt to save ourselves, becomes the ceiling of our spiritual cage, an addiction.

Like the sparrow, in futility, but repeatedly, we try to get out the top, to save ourselves. Eventually, we find our misguided self-sufficiency not only does not work, but the continual efforts exhaust us to the point of developing serious health concerns. Only when we exhaust ourselves like that sparrow, hit bottom, get "sick and tired of being sick and tired" will we be able to realize or accept that there is a small open door waiting for us at the bottom, a door called "humility."

It is that door, and that door only, that will take us out of our cage and on to a healing journey that we will explore in Part Four, a journey that leads to a new life of sobriety, where we may be happy and free.

Our Spiritual Burden

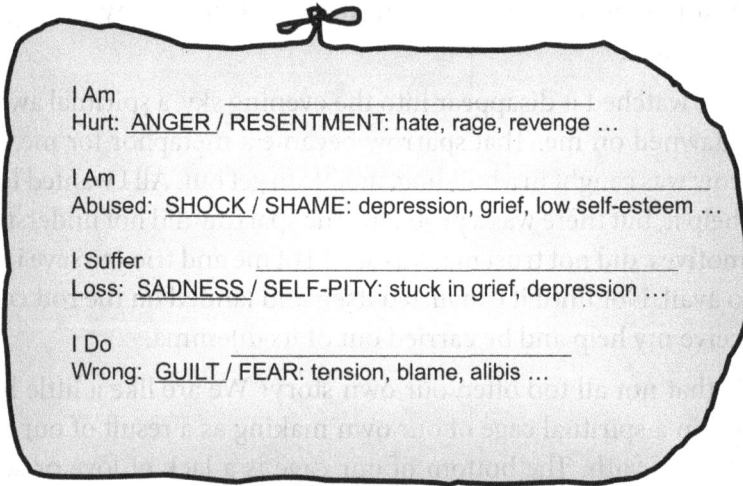

Illustration 12

Another way of describing the phenomenon of the spiritual cage is by exploring the metaphor of the spiritual garbage bag that many people carry through life. We begin that description with a short story.

Two monks, an older monk and a novice, were walking along, returning to the monastery. As they approached a creek, they saw a beautiful woman waiting there for help to cross. Out of deference, she asked the older monk if he would carry her across. He declined, saying they had a rule not to touch a woman. Undeterred, she asked the younger monk if he would carry her across. He agreed, picked her up, carried her across and put her down on the shore. She went on her way, and the two monks continued back to the monastery.

As they walked along, it was obvious that the older monk was quite troubled and disturbed. The younger monk, however, was whistling, smiling and clearly enjoying himself. Finally, the older monk asked his companion, "Don't you know that it is against the rules to touch a woman?" The younger monk replied that he did. After a few minutes of silent walking, the older monk, still troubled, asked the younger monk, "Why did you pick up that woman and carry her across, then? Don't you feel guilty that you broke the rules?" The younger monk replied, "Brother, I picked her up, carried her across and put her down. You're still carrying her!"

This story describes the lived reality of all too many people today, carrying an invisible garbage bag, a spiritual burden, through life. This invisible garbage bag carries all one's hurt, anger, guilt and pain, and is so overloaded and heavy that, with the slightest touch or repositioning, the one carrying it erupts when crossed, perceives to be crossed, or suffers a hurtful word.

To help understand the power and the process involved in working Steps Four through Nine, the core of the program, one must grasp the nature of the spiritual burden these steps will address, and how they are designed to heal. *Illustration 12* is a graphic illustration of this spiritual burden that threatens to overwhelm the one carrying it.

To explain this schema in a little more detail, consider the following. When one is hurt in any way, the first reaction will be *anger*, which, if repressed and not addressed, will turn into resentment. Given time, this resentment will evolve into various forms or shades of a desire for revenge, hatred, cynicism, even rage, as well as a host of other painful emotions.

This idea of anger morphing into resentment is echoed by John Monbourquette, who writes, "Resentment is a form of disguised anger that festers around a badly healed wound. Anger is a healthy emotion that disappears once it has been expressed; resentment and hostility settle in as defensive attitudes that are always ready to respond to real or imagined onslaughts."[33]

If the hurt is extreme (such as the trauma involved in sexual abuse), then one's reaction will be more extreme, such as *shock*. Shock can happen to anyone at any time. An example is what happens after a child falls down a set of stairs, followed by silence and the fear that the child is hurt or perhaps dead. The parent runs down the stairs, picks up the child, embraces him and checks him out quickly. Then and only then does the child start to cry. That child was in shock. The fall was too sudden, unexpected and abrupt for the child to comprehend or react to. The child goes into shock, not knowing if it is safe to even cry, until he is held by loving arms and knows that it is safe to do so.

The shock of trauma can lead an individual into a sense of shame, especially if the victim is young. Because parents are idolized and can do no wrong in the eyes of their children, the children often blame themselves. "Something must be wrong with me for my mom or dad or a trusted adult to do that to me," they reason. They begin to experience shame, which is not the same as guilt. Guilt is a realization that I have done something wrong. Guilt can be a healthy emotion, leading to admission of wrongdoing, forgiveness and healing. Shame, on the other hand, is a very complex and painful emotion that says that something is wrong with me, that I am bad. This can be devastating, leading to feelings of depression, low self-worth and, eventually, toxic shame that may poison a person's whole outlook on life.

Every hurt also involves a loss. It might be loss of a relationship, self-esteem, reputation, dignity, innocence, joy or myriad losses. This loss leads naturally to a feeling of *sadness*, which, if not addressed, will go underground and become self-pity that, in turn, becomes various degrees of grief, depression, loneliness, loss of trust, etc. People often get stuck in grief, unable to move on with their lives or deal with their loss, some even to the point of ending their lives.

Many people, especially the young, simply do not know how to deal with all this hurt in a positive way. They react out of anger by striking back or striking out, doing wrong to others and hurting them, often just for the sake of hurting someone or destroying some object. This, of course, leads to a feeling of *guilt*, even if it is never admitted. This guilt eventually morphs into a sense of fear that spills out into all kinds of tension, denial of wrongdoing, and a need to blame others, as well as a host of other feelings and emotions that all add up to an invisible spiritual burden.

Looking over the pattern of the journey into addiction in *Illustration 10*, I don't think anyone is completely on one side or the other. We drift back and forth, but one side will predominate. And if we are on the side of addiction, there is hope. The Twelve Steps, if we choose to work them, are like a glove fitting this pattern and taking us through it to new freedom. The choice is ours. We can remain stuck in grief, or move on to healthy grieving and recovery using the Twelve Steps, a way that works if we work it. We turn our attention next to exploring the Twelve Step healing journey.

Suggested Activities

1. Review Part Three and pray for the grace to be open to recognizing any of the areas that speak to your journey in life. Place a checkmark by them, and when you have finished, make a list from what you have checked off. Take your list to prayer.

2. Sit down with a friend you truly trust and value, perhaps your soulmate, and share your personal journey with that person. No one should be alone on this journey.

QUESTION FOR REFLECTION

1. Where do you see God's presence in your life to be very active? Where do you still see the need for healing?

PART FOUR: **The Twelve Step Healing Journey**

The Twelve Step program of Alcoholics Anonymous is a self-help program that has stood the test of time and has spawned many other support groups for other addictions. Over the course of giving workshops and retreats for many years, I have adapted the steps to accommodate other fellowships, such as Al-Anon, Adult Children of Alcoholics (ACOA) and Co-dependents Anonymous (CoDA). Permission to do so was obtained from the Central Office of Alcoholics Anonymous World Services in New York City, provided that the original steps and a disclaimer were included. These can be found in the appendix to this book.

Given that permission, the adapted steps are listed below, with the adaptations in italics. I also found it helpful to entitle each step.

The Twelve Steps of Alcoholics Anonymous Adapted

1. Humility and Powerlessness:

We admitted we were powerless over alcohol *(others)* – that our lives had become unmanageable.

2. Faith:

Came to believe that a Power greater than ourselves could restore us to sanity.

3. Surrender:

Made a decision to turn our will and our lives over to the care of God as we understood *God*.

4. Honesty:

Made a searching and fearless moral inventory of ourselves.

5. Trust:

Admitted to God, to ourselves, and to another human being the exact nature of our wrongs.

6. Forgiveness:

Were entirely ready to have God remove all these defects of character.

7. Healing:

Humbly asked *God* to remove our shortcomings *and fill us with the gifts of the Holy Spirit.*

8. Courage:

Made a list of all persons we had harmed, and became willing to make amends to them all.

9. Reconciliation:

Made direct amends to such people wherever possible, except when to do so would injure them or others.

10. Awareness:

Continued to take personal inventory, and when we were wrong, promptly admitted it.

11. Prayer:

Sought through prayer and meditation to improve our conscious contact with God as we understood *God*, praying only for the knowledge of *God's* will for us and the power to carry that out.

12. Sharing and Service:

Having had a spiritual awakening as the result of these steps, we tried to carry this message to alcoholics *(others)*, and to practice these principles in all our affairs.

The adaptations are few and simple. In Step One and Step Twelve, "*others*" is added to include all members of other fellowships that also use the Twelve Steps. The pronoun *"Him"* is replaced with *"God"* wherever it occurs, to be more inclusive.

A glance at Step Seven in the appendix will reveal that I added the words *and fill us with the gifts of the Holy Spirit* to that step. There is a simple reason for this addition. The easiest way to get air out of an empty glass is not to use a vacuum pump, but rather to fill the glass with water to push out the air. In a similar manner, I believe that God does not so much pull our character defects out of us as much as God simply fills us with the gifts of the Spirit that heal our painful emotions and transform our defects of character into positive virtues such as faith, hope, love, patience, forgiveness, etc.

With these adapted steps, we now commence a Twelve Step healing journey.

The Twelve Step Healing Journey

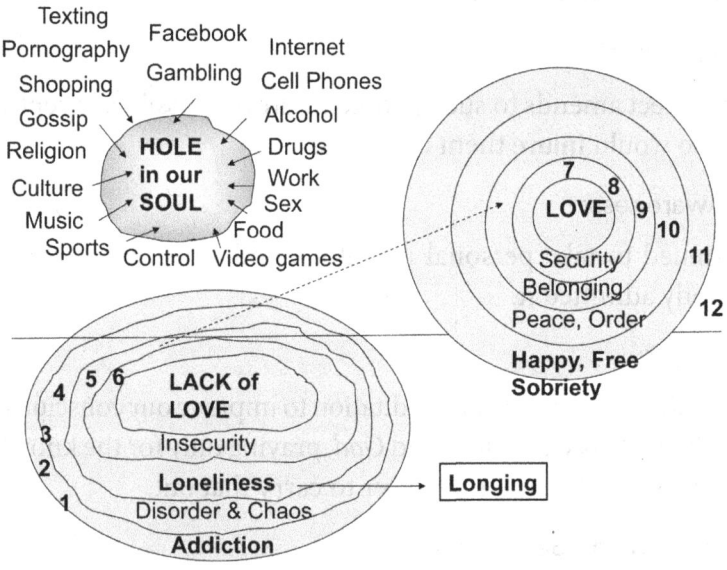

Illustration 13

We have explored the mystery of being human, a spirituality of recovery and wellness, and the journey into addiction. The question that begs a response at the outset of this healing journey is this: How do we move forward to find happy, free sobriety?

I believe that the Twelve Step program of Alcoholics Anonymous is a reliable and trustworthy way available to us. Working these steps will take us on a spiritual journey from addiction, through our past, to a new future of happy, free sobriety. There is a chapter in the Big Book entitled "How It Works." Relating the steps to our Beach Balls image in *Illustration 13* is simply an application of the contents of that chapter.

Step One is placed at the bottom left corner of the Lack of Love Ball, beside the word "addiction," because the starting point for healing is to admit that we are powerless over something in our lives and that our life is unmanageable.

Step Two is placed next to and slightly above Step One on the Lack of Love Ball, and indicates some movement towards healing by coming to a new expression of faith. This step acknowledges growth of belief in a Higher Power that can restore us to sanity.

We can look at our lives and see how lack of love, weak faith and our own attempts to save ourselves led us into addiction and self-destruction. We are ready to let go of these futile attempts to save ourselves, and to try this new path that allows the Big Book to boldly claim, "Rarely have we seen a person fail who has thoroughly followed our path."[34]

Step Three is placed next to and slightly above Step Two, indicating more movement towards healing by acting on our growing faith in God, instead of acting out of our repressed emotions and hurt. Step Three is a leap of faith. We move deeper into our own life experience, with God and towards love, instead of apart from God and away from love.

Step Four moves us into the circle of chaos and disorder and how we tried to save ourselves through defence mechanisms and coping skills. We ultimately realize that we didn't so much *save* ourselves as merely *survive,* and did so at the cost of hurting many people. We are now asked to take a hard look at the chaos in our lives, our disorder, and all the ways that we acted out and hurt others in our misguided attempt to protect ourselves from more hurt. The search is exhaustive, and our moral inventory needs to be fearless and brutally honest.

Step Five takes us into the circle of dealing with and ridding ourselves of our terrible loneliness by sharing our story and especially by revealing our dark secrets with a trusted other. More than that, we are achieving a deep degree of intimacy, perhaps for the first time in our lives.

Step Six takes us to the heart of our hurt and our wounded self, dealing with and facing our primary defect of character, human insecurity and all the other defects that flow from that. We realize our need not only for forgiveness, but also for inner healing.

Step Seven is a quantum leap into the healing experience of God's unconditional love through prayer. As we commune with our Higher Power in Step Seven prayer, we begin to let go of our hurt and resentment by forgiving those who hurt us, forgiving ourselves and accepting our losses. We are now beginning to love and to be loved, realizing that it is love and only love that can heal us. We are beginning to come alive and experience new life and energy.

Steps Eight and Nine take us into the circles of security and belonging and further along our path to meeting our deepest human needs to be loved and to belong. We are starting to feel that we belong to the human race once again as we slowly and courageously begin to reach out to the people we harmed, listen to them, soak up their pain and apologize to them one by one. We try to make up for the harm we caused them by seeking to make amends in whatever way we can, and we make a declaration never to act in that hurtful way again. We can sense the beginnings of healthy friendships and relationships.

Step Ten moves us into the circle of order and peace, as we daily monitor our progress and make corrections and apologies when necessary.

Step Eleven places us in the circle of happy, free sobriety supported by prayer. This spiritual experience will grow daily through meditation and prayer as we mature in our relationship with God, who is love.

Step Twelve places us outside the Love Ball on the surface of the water, as we are called to reach out and share with others the healing we have received. We have been transformed from miserable and enslaved addicts to happy, free, loving human beings, thanks to the Twelve Steps. We now have the "bounce" we need to face and deal with life's problems as they come our way, instead of desperately trying to avoid them and to numb out the pain that can come from being human.

That "bounce" is what Terrence Gorski describes as he writes, "Recovery is the process of trading in one set of problems for a better set of problems. The more advanced we are in recovery, the more able we are to cope with problems. Successful recovery does not mean being problem free; it means being better able to cope with problems that are presented to us in our recovery without becoming upset."[35]

Working these steps, we come continually closer to realizing in our lives that beautiful saying of St. Irenaeus mentioned in Part One, "The glory of God is man (and woman) fully alive."

There we have it: happy, free sobriety by working the Twelve Steps, in place of destructive, agonizing addiction. They work if we work them. And now let us take a closer look at how they work.

A. Getting into the Program (Steps One – Three)

STEP ONE: Humility and Powerlessness

We admitted we were powerless over alcohol (others) –
that our lives had become unmanageable.

They were wandering in the desert, in the wastelands,
could find no way to an inhabited city;
they were hungry and thirsty,
their life was ebbing away. (Psalm 107:4-5)

*

The foundation of a new house is not made of rocks. It is made of grey powder from crushed rock that is purchased in bags, mixed with gravel and water, resulting in concrete, that amazing material that is used to build skyscrapers and overpasses.

It is the same with us. If we are hard as rocks – proud, stubborn, resisting help, denying that we have any problems – then we will not change or grow. We may be physically present in rehabilitation centres or in other programs, but nothing will happen in our minds and hearts if they are hard and impenetrable, like rocks.

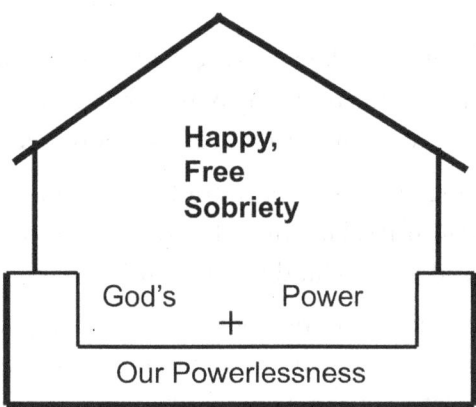

Illustration 14

What we want for ourselves is a new life of happy, free sobriety. But to achieve that goal, that new life, we need a foundation. We need to become aware of our brokenness and to be made into that grey powder used to make concrete. It is our weakness, our brokenness, our powerlessness that God wants and can use to build new lives. Then the water of God's power can mix with the gravel and powder of our powerlessness, and a foundation open to transformation will emerge. A life of happy, free sobriety can be built on that foundation, the foundation of humble powerlessness. Humility and powerlessness are the best foundation for a new life.

This admission of powerlessness, however, goes contrary to every instinct in our bodies. We react to hurt by self-preservation, striving for control, protection and personal power over others. Perhaps that is why it is so difficult for some of us to "hit bottom," sometimes destroying our families and even ourselves in the process, before admitting that we are powerless over something in our lives. Admitting powerlessness is the most solid basis for change, healing and transformation. Happy are those who can stop trying to find a softer, easier way, who can humbly admit powerlessness and can reach out for help.

How sad it is to witness someone who simply will not or cannot admit powerlessness and reach out for this help. I remember visiting a hospitalized middle-aged alcoholic. He was bloated and barely coherent. As I left the room, I said to him, "Thomas, I hope to see you again," to which he muttered in a low voice, "Don't tell anyone I'm here." That comment almost broke my heart. Dying of cirrhosis of the liver, he was still too proud to admit that he was an alcoholic and needed help. He passed away a few weeks later, leaving behind his wife and four young children. I could not help but wonder how different his life could have been had he been able to do even Step One.

I suspect that we all know persons who appear to be blind to their own condition and unable to see how powerfully they are caught in an addiction or a character defect, hurting themselves and their loved ones. Concerned intervention – also described as "raising a person's bottom" – is a method that can be employed to help those who are resisting the truth of their own addiction. A brief description of this method is provided in the appendix to this book.

In the end, Step One consists of simply admitting our brokenness, our need for help, and then humbly asking others for that help. We may be powerless over something more powerful than we are, but we are not helpless. We can do something by admitting our own truth and reaching out for help. In terms of mental wellness, we need to face reality, accept reality and deal with reality, and Step One can help us do that.

There is a saying: "The truth may hurt, but it will set us free." Someone quipped that the truth will set us free, but first it will make us miserable. There may be some truth to this, but the bottom line is that our humble admission of powerlessness becomes the foundation on which, with God's help, we can build a new life of happy, free sobriety.

STEP TWO: Faith

Came to believe that a Power greater than ourselves could restore us to sanity.

Because it is by grace that you have been saved, through faith; not by anything of your own, but by a gift from God.
(Ephesians 2:7-10)

*

The background for understanding this step is very much the pattern of our "Original Wound" or "Core Grief," discussed earlier, which caused us to lose our faith in our Higher Power in the first place.

"Came to believe"

Step Two begins with *belief*. Belief is largely an intellectual act, something that happens in our heads. We believe in all kinds of things and facts: that our car will start when we turn the key, that our alarm will ring when we set it to go off in the morning and that the plane we board will take us safely to our destination. Yes, we believe in all kinds of persons, facts and things.

To be effective in our lives, however, our belief must move towards *faith*. Faith is more personal. We place our faith in a person, in someone, and not just in facts or things. Our faith is then called to grow even stronger, to become *trust*. We believe in the goodness of another person. We begin to have faith that this person will live up to their promises, and we express that faith by sharing who we are more deeply with others. But it does not end there. Our trust is then challenged to become *surrender*, to actually place our lives in the other person's hands. That trust is expressed by some action, such as sharing our feelings with him or her. The whole process of Step Two is a dynamic movement from belief, through faith and trust, to complete surrender that takes us to Step Three.

Step Two, then, becomes crucial. Little by little, with more experience, and putting behind us coping skills and defence mechanisms that really didn't work, we can now go about renewing our faith in God and trusting in God once again.

Perhaps a little story will help illustrate the point. A young man once asked his friends if they believed that he could push a wheelbarrow on a high wire over Niagara Falls. Of course they said, "No. No one could do that." He proceeded to take the rubber off the wheel and push the wheelbarrow, on the wire, over the falls and back again. Then he asked his friends, "Now do you believe that I can push a wheelbarrow on a high wire over Niagara Falls?" They answered, "Yes, we believe you can do that." He asked them again, "Do you really believe that I can push a wheelbarrow on a cable over Niagara Falls?" They replied, "Yes, we just saw you do it; we believe you can." "All right," he replied, "if you really believe I can do that, who will be the first? Get in and I'll give you a ride!"

This story, to which there may be some truth, since one person did walk a high wire over the falls in recent years, captures the essence of Step Two: coming to believe that a Higher Power can work in our lives. Needless to say, this man's offer for a free ride across the falls had no takers among his friends.

Getting into the wheelbarrow is quite a different reality than simply observing the feat and believing that it can be done. Steps Two and Three ask us not only to believe that a miracle can happen within us, but to act on that faith, to trust enough to get into God's wheelbarrow and go for the ride.

The words of Jesus "Truly I tell you, unless you change and become like children, you will never enter the kingdom of heaven" (Matthew 18:3) take on new meaning in the light of Step Two. Whenever I throw a little child up in the air and see it laughing, totally trusting that I will catch it on the way down, I marvel at that kind of childlike trust.

I also feel moved to realize that is the kind of trust we are called to in Step Two to be able to move on into healing.

That a Power greater than ourselves

Another Step Two image might be a trapper's cabin situated under a power line in the forest. Though the cabin is close to a huge amount of power, that power is of no use to the trapper or his TV, electric stove and other appliances unless there is a transformer, a line into the cabin and a switch or plug-in on the wall. In this image, the power line can represent our Higher Power; the transformer becomes the Twelve Steps and the line into the cabin is the fellowship of support groups and the role of prayer in our lives. Faith expressed through prayer is how we turn the switch on and plug ourselves into accessing God's power.

"Restore us to sanity"

Step Two also calls us to some honest humility. We need to look honestly at our behaviour and lifestyle, and realize how crazy it has all become, how little sense it makes. I find myself pointing out to people struggling with this step how irrational their behaviour is and how damaging it is to themselves and their families. In the end, our behaviour is crazy and insane when it can be seen for what it is.

My personal experience of this step in restoring my sanity spans two decades, and it involved two major crises in my life. A stressful ministry situation as a priest caused me to escape into more and more work at the cost of leisure and relationships. This was what the program would call insanity. Already burned out when I was made provincial of our Oblate province, I was overwhelmed and had to resign, leading to months of therapy to heal.

The pattern repeated itself when I was named an archbishop. Without being aware of it, I began to work harder and harder, again at the cost of leisure and relationships. The insanity this time took the form of not listening to concerned individuals who were trying to point out what was happening, that I was burning out. It also took the form of an inability to make changes in my lifestyle and ministry. Again, I crashed and burned, and needed months of therapy to heal.

During this time of renewal, I finally realized with clarity the particular insanity of my behaviour and my need to, once again, even as a minister of religion, find the God whom I could trust with my life to restore me to sanity. It is this experience and awareness that finally brought me home to the fellowship of Workaholics Anonymous (WA) that a group of us began in Edmonton in January 2015.

Step Two seeks to move us beyond intellectual belief, to personal faith in God once again. We are asked to put our faith and trust not just in the existence of a Higher Power, but in a Higher Power who can restore us to sanity, who will actually work in our lives, and begin to transform and heal us.

STEP THREE: Surrender

Made a decision to turn our lives and our wills over to the care of God as we understood God.

We have recognized for ourselves,
and put our faith in, the love God has for us.
God is love, and whoever remains in love,
remains in God. (1 John 4:16)

*

A man hiking on a mountain fell off a cliff. Halfway down, he managed to grab hold of a branch. Looking up, he realized how far he had fallen. Looking down, he could see cars like ants on the winding highway far below. Suspended between heaven and earth and quickly getting tired, he decided to call for help at the top of his lungs, "Is anybody up there?" A deep voice answered, "Yes, I am up here." Surprised and relieved, he asked, "Who are you?" The voice replied, "I am God." "Wow – what luck!" the man thought to himself, and then cried out, "If you are God, can you get me out of here?" The voice responded, "Yes, I can. Have faith, let go of the branch, and I will take you to safety." The man looked down, saw once again how far it was, and then looked up, only to see how far he had already fallen. "Have faith, let go of the branch," he repeated, trying to convince himself, and he tried to let go of the branch, but couldn't. Then he cried out in desperation, "Is anybody else up there?"

This little story neatly captures the challenge of Step Three: making a decision to surrender our lives to God as we understand God. This is much easier to talk about than to actually do, and as a result, many people get stuck on Step Three, finding it difficult to move on. There is a need to explore any avenue that might make trusting and surrendering to God more feasible, so let us explore this step to plumb its meaning and power to impact our recovery.

Made a decision

The Marriage Encounter movement teaches us that "Love is a decision." Step Three invites us to grow in our ability to love God by trusting God more deeply and by making a willing act of faith in God, for the sake of finding a new life for ourselves.

Step Three calls for a decision that one may not feel like making. It is a call to a mature approach to life. It is an invitation to refuse to be controlled by one's feelings or to numb out those feelings. It is a call to rise to a higher level of human existence: to decide to take the positive action that is necessary for one's continued growth and healing. This action is to surrender one's life and will to the care of God.

To turn over our will and our lives

With this step, we are being asked to turn our will and our life over to the care of God, to surrender the deepest part of our being. From the powerlessness of Step One to the deeper faith expressed through complete trust of Step Two, this Step is a call to action, to let go, to trust as we have never trusted before, to step out into the unknown with faith.

It is no accident that the basic movement that underlies the Judeo-Christian faith was Abraham's journey into the unknown, when he left behind the familiar and the secure, trusting that God would reveal his destination to him on the way (Genesis 12:1).

It is this kind of raw faith and courage that Step Three calls for. Surrendering our life and our will is a journey of faith. At the same time, surrendering our life is perhaps the simpler of the two. After all, we all must die someday, so making this step simply becomes a symbolic way of prefiguring this inevitable experience.

But what of one's will? The fact that we have been given free will as a gift from God, a gift that God totally and absolutely respects, perhaps makes this part of the step the most difficult.

Who of us can say that we have never struggled with self-will or stubbornness or control? This special gift of free will is, in some respects, stronger than death itself. It is this gift that enables us to sacrifice our lives for the sake of a higher cause. Negatively, it is also this gift that, when abused, will lead people to harm and even to kill others or themselves in a variety of ways.

Step Three asks us to have the faith and trust in God to take that deepest part of our human reality, that most precious gift of our will that we have been given, and give it back to God as we understand God. Our will is what truly distinguishes us from animals that operate out of instinct.

This gift is a double-edged sword, however. The lack of love in our lives in the past has led us to misuse our free will for stubborn self-sufficiency. We have used it to doggedly try to save ourselves, only to find ourselves in the throes of addiction.

One resident at a treatment centre joined a Codependents Anonymous group that met at that facility – without the permission of the treatment team – because he thought they were not putting him in enough modalities. When his condition worsened, he was confronted by his therapist as to why he had never questioned the reason the team had not encouraged him to join the group. When he finally did ask, he was shocked to discover that the treatment team found him not codependent at all, but rather quite independent and even stubborn about doing the program his own way. His stubborn self-sufficiency was actually slowing down his healing. When that became clear to him, he ate humble pie, changed his attitude, and his healing improved markedly.

In this step, we are being asked to surrender, to let go of this survival skill of stubborn self-sufficiency that we have relied upon. We are being asked to turn our stubborn self-will over to God, to let go of this crutch so we can begin, however hesitantly, to do God's will in our lives.

We need to overcome our fear of losing ourselves and our identity. If we are able to do this, we will experience the mysterious truth that it is in giving ourselves away that we will find ourselves.

For those who find Step Three daunting, it might be good to point out the difference between the words *surrender* and *succumb*. *Surrender* is when we take on another's request of us as though it were our own. *Succumb* is when we respond to a request with resentment and victimhood.

To help us appreciate the nature of this genuine surrender, we turn to Gerald May, who writes,

> True spiritual surrender ... rather than promising continuation of control and autonomy ... poses giving up the reins and freely choosing to acknowledge one's utter ultimate dependency. True surrender offers none of the usual ego-gratifications. It cannot be seen as a "last noble act." There is nothing of traditional heroism in it. There is no noise or fanfare. It is done—*must* be done—quietly in the deepest recess of one's own heart. It cannot be used to escape from responsibility. It cannot be a way of avoiding pain. It cannot be a means of getting what one wants or expressing one's anger. It cannot be an avoidance of anything. Instead, it involves a moving into life as it is given, with all of its joy and suffering, pleasure and pain.[36]

Hopefully, these words will help those who are wavering to be able to let go of their stubborn self-will. But what of our lives? How does one turn their life over to God?

Actually, the answer is very simple – do Steps Four and Five. The best way that I know to turn one's life over to God is to take a picture of that life and give that picture away to someone else. And that is what Steps Four and Five are all about: undertaking a searching and fearless inventory of our whole life, and then giving that life to God by sharing it with another human being.

The God of Our Understanding

A Chinese gentleman once came up to a missionary and said, "Reverend Father, I have no trouble understanding God the Father, and I have no trouble understanding God the Son, but I am finding it difficult to understand the Honourable Bird!"

His dilemma is perhaps a reflection of the struggle many people have with this step, especially in terms of settling on an image or concept of God with which they can be comfortable.

As we have seen earlier, past hurts or wounds make it difficult for some people to even believe in a Higher Power or God at all, let alone consider turning their lives over to a Higher Power. Others have had negative experiences with their church that make it difficult for them to have a positive relationship with God. Still others may be reacting against a negative concept of God that they have been wrongly taught. Since deciding to surrender one's life to God or a Higher Power hangs greatly on one's image of God or that Higher Power, it seems logical to explore the images of God that we might have.

Any brainstorming of images of God typically yields words such as the following: Creator, Almighty, Powerful, Father, Love, Punishing, Fearful, Awesome, Merciful, Forgiving, Omnipresent, etc. One image that has rarely surfaced during a brainstorming session is "Family."

One day I was visiting a couple when their 15-year-old daughter returned from a soccer tournament in a nearby city. She burst into the house, threw down her equipment bag, went straight to where her father was sitting, plopped herself on his lap, threw her arm around his neck, rested her head against his, and remained there motionless for some minutes, soaking up his love.

The father continued our conversation without missing a beat. His wife kept on preparing supper, while the other children played quietly in the background. This appeared to be normal in this household, but I was transfixed at this sight of loving closeness between a father and daughter. The daughter was soaking up the tender, intimate love that the father was offering. That picture stayed with me for days. As I reflected on it and on my reaction to it, I realized that I had been privileged to see a glimpse of what God is like.

Illustration 15 is an attempt to share with you what is now my preferred image of God as family, partly as a result of that experience. I do so not wanting to impose my spirituality on anyone, but simply in the spirit of "God as I understand God." If this image helps you, then use it. If it is not helpful, then feel free to skip this part and move on.

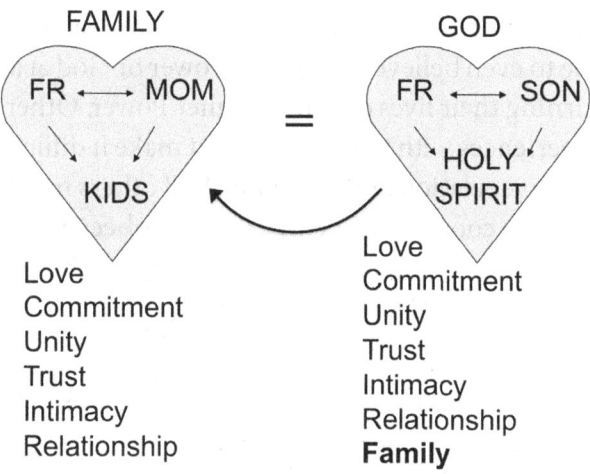

Illustration 15

What I saw in that home was a father and a mother who had made a decision to love, and who were playing that decision out. Theirs is a committed marriage relationship, so that love is permanent. Their mutual love produced children who are the product of that love and included in that love. There was love, commitment, unity, trust, intimacy and relationship in that family.

God our Father/Mother is the source of all life and love, and, as Father or loving parent, gives God's self totally to the Son and eternally "births" the Son. The Son is totally receptive to the Father's love, and as Son, reflects back the Father's love through humble obedience. The bond of love flowing between them is the Holy Spirit, much like the love relationship that bonds a husband and wife together.

This Trinitarian love is also a committed relationship, just like a marriage, only eternal – it always was and always will be. So for me now, just like that family, God is love, commitment, unity, trust, intimacy, relationship and family beyond imagining.

This is an image of God that I can identify with and to which I can relate. For me, it is very human and personal, warm and approachable. This ideal image of God as family, of course, could never be fully realized by humans, who are limited and imperfect. However, we are invited to move towards healing our own families and becoming more like the family of God in how we live and move and relate to one another. And we are given the gift of the Holy Spirit to help us move in that direction.

This has been my experience with my own family. There was not that much intimacy or closeness, especially as I entered my teenage years, but as we grew older and started understanding that healing was possible, we have made great strides to heal and transform our family, including holding a family retreat.

After the death of both our parents, I invited my siblings to gather for a day of family healing at the old farmhouse where we grew up. We began by sharing our stories to catch up on each other's experience and history during the years when we had drifted apart.

We then did some family imagery. Each person shared their image of our family with the others. Some said we had been like canoes drifting along in a stream, sometimes bumping into each other. One compared us to a broken pottery vase that we were trying to put back together. For another, we were like a wagon wheel that had a hub and spokes, but no rim holding the spokes together.

We shared our feelings about where we were at in this stage of our lives, and we asked forgiveness from one another for any hurts from the past. We then celebrated the Eucharist together, and finished the day with a family meal. The result was increased intimacy, closeness and sharing of affection among us.

But what if the historical hurts and deep divisions seem insurmountable, and there is little possibility of communication, as in the case of severely dysfunctional families, broken families, or instances where there have been generations of sexual abuse and incest?

A Compassionate Higher Power

In this context, there is another image of God that I find helpful and would like to share with you. I acknowledge and respect the possibility that this image of God may be unacceptable or inconceivable to some readers. I posit this image of God as one I find comforting, but certainly accept the reader's decision to ignore this image if it seems inappropriate, especially when persons or families are struggling with deep historical hurts linked with faith or religion.

When things don't work out in my life, or when I am hurt and abused, this Higher Power understands because He has experienced it and dealt with it in the best way possible – forgiveness. *(Hebrews 4:14-16)*

Illustration 16

This image comes from a Step Five workshop held to help prepare clergy, counsellors and pastoral workers to do Step Five. Don C., a retired Anglican priest, was the main facilitator. At one point, he claimed that Jesus had probably been sexually abused. Initially, I was shocked to hear that assertion. However, the more I considered it and learned about how crucifixions were done in Roman times, the more that assertion appeared probable.

For the Romans, crucifixion was a method of capital punishment intended to inflict the maximum excruciating pain and humiliation on the criminal. Sometimes victims were hung upside down. If the crime was of a sexual nature, the genitals might also be nailed to the cross. When Jesus was stripped, flogged, mocked and humiliated, is it not possible that the soldiers also abused him sexually? News reports of soldiers inflicting sexual abuse on prisoners in the Iraq war lend credence to this view.

I usually share this theory with sexual abuse victims, particularly those who cry out in anguish, "Where was God when this abuse happened to me?" The answer is stark and powerful: God, in Christ, was there with them, experiencing the same abuse that they were experiencing. On the cross, Jesus both suffers and knows what it is to be an innocent victim.

God did not prevent his Son from suffering the abuse, torture and humiliation inflicted upon him. Nor did God prevent his painful death on the cross. In like manner, God does not prevent our abuse and trauma. What God does is share that pain and abuse with us, fully and totally. There is a mystery here of how deep love works. We are invited to set aside our normal way of thinking and open ourselves up to that mystery.

The power of this mystery is that Jesus chose to respond to the evil and pain inflicted on him in a totally non-violent manner, with forgiveness. "Like a sheep being led to slaughter," as the scriptures put it in Isaiah 53:7, he submitted and chose not to fight, nor flee, nor freeze, but to rely on his faith in God's love to deliver him, even from the death that would ensue.

Scripture states that from the cross Jesus cried out to God, "Father, forgive them; for they do not know what they are doing" (Luke 23:34). Even he did not trust his own strength, but turned to the Father and trusted that the Father would raise him up, as indeed happened on Easter Sunday morning. We are asked to have that same kind of faith and to choose to respond to our own hurt as he did, non-violently and with forgiveness instead of bitterness or resentment.

The depth of this faithful love is revealed even more poignantly as Jesus appears to his fearful friends in the upper room, behind locked doors (John 20:19-23). "Peace be with you," he says, and shows them his hands and side, forgiving those who had denied and abandoned him. There is no anger, no resentment, no desire for revenge, just peace and joy flowing from his love and forgiveness that alone breaks the cycle of violence that even today holds the world in its curse. He still bore the scars, as do we. We cannot change the past. We cannot undo the fact that we have been hurt, raped, abused, cheated, called down and beaten. We can't forget that these things have happened to us, for the scars and the memories continue to exist.

However, with this step, we don't have to try to forget, as we have so often tried to do, by turning to anything that might medicate, alleviate or block out our pain. No, now a new way is open for us, the way of forgiveness. In fact, Jesus commanded us to do as he has done and has given us the power to do it, as he breathes on us the same Spirit that transformed the fearful disciples into courageous bearers of this Good News to all peoples since then. It is this power to forgive and to break the cycle of violence that we will explore in greater depth in Steps Six and Seven.

I never cease to marvel at how the program works for all, no matter what their concept of God is. Perhaps more than any other, this one phrase, *as we understood God*, underlies the magnanimity of our God, who isn't fussy over what God is called or how God is understood, as we wounded and hurt human beings begin our journey back to God as we understand God.

The bottom line for progress, healing, growth and moving on with the other Steps seems to be the ability to trust at least some power greater than ourselves. God's overriding concern is that people begin to heal.

As Richard Rohr points out in his talks, God is very patient. If God was willing to watch dinosaurs eat grass for millions of years, God must also be in no hurry to pressure us to come to a clear, definitive concept of who God is before starting to heal us and renew us.

This also is the beauty and magnanimity of the Twelve Step program. Each person can begin to work Step Three with whatever understanding they have of God, and to experience the power of the program. I have seen people whose images of God vary from the air itself to a friend or their support group celebrate Step Five and experience growth and healing.

Whatever one's image of God, the Big Book offers a prayer for Step Three: "God, I offer myself to Thee – to build with me and to do with me as Thou wilt. Relieve me of the bondage of self, that I may better do Thy will. Take away my difficulties, that victory over them may bear witness to those I would help of Thy Power, Thy Love, and Thy Way of life. May I do Thy will always!"[37]

For me, God is no longer an aloof power who will protect me from all suffering and harm. God shares my suffering, and will give me the strength to live through my difficulties. God can and will draw good out of the most negative situations I might find myself in. This belief reminds me of the popular meditation called *Footprints*. Where there are two sets of footprints, we are walking with God. Where there is only one set of footprints, God is carrying us, suffering with and in us.

This takes us to the end of the first major division of the Steps. A saying sums up Steps One, Two and Three this way: "I came; I came to; I came to believe." Another saying is "I can't; He can. I'll let Him." Now, as we wrap up this discussion on Step Three, it is with the realization that the next two steps, Four and Five, are the steps that actualize and enflesh Step Three and get us into the meat of the program, so let's turn our attention to them now.

B. The Heart of the Program (Steps Four to Nine)

STEP FOUR: Honesty

Made a searching and fearless inventory of ourselves.

And so now they are steeped in all kinds of injustice, rottenness, greed and malice; full of envy, murder, wrangling, treachery and spite, libellers, slanderers, enemies of God, rude, arrogant and boastful, enterprising in evil, rebellious to parents, without brains, honour, love or pity. (Romans 1:29-30)

*

We have now arrived at a pivotal part of the program, Steps Four to Nine. As mentioned earlier, the meat of the program begins with Step Four.

Getting Started on Step Four

The hardest part of doing Step Four is just getting started, since the task seems monumental. A simple way to begin is to use the Medicine Wheel. Recall the four life stages of the Medicine Wheel: child, youth, adult and elder. For young adults, the stages could become child, youth, young adulthood and the present time.

The key to doing Step Four is to begin to *remember*. Remembering is the antithesis of addiction, which tries to forget the past, block out memories and medicate the pain. We must begin to remember and to relive the past, however painful it was and might still be. Remembering is the key to healing.

A second key to doing Step Four well and to healing is to allow ourselves to feel the pain and stay with the emotions. Remember, we cannot heal what we cannot feel. The temptation will always be to stop, to run away and to avoid the pain. This is what led us into addiction in the first place. Here the words of the Big Book really hit home: "We thought we could find an easier, softer way."[38] In reality, there is no other way. The basic truth of healing is that the only way through the pain is through the pain.

It is important to remember that we do not do this alone. We have our Higher Power who has been through it before and conquered the emotional pain. Whatever happened to us happened to Him, and He will help us handle it now. We also have a sponsor with whom we can share the pain, as well as our group and the meetings. The support is there. All we need is the commitment to work this step.

One way of doing a Step Four might be penning an autobiography. Someone once said that the unexamined life is not worth living. A jokester turned that around to say that the unlived life is not worth examining. All joking aside, Step Four is all about examining one's life. It is a deep, profound examination of conscience. Done right, it is a gruelling application of sandpaper on the varnish of our outside self to get at the inner core of our life.

This step speaks of an inventory that is a moral inventory, not just an immoral inventory. We are complex people; we have failings, but we also have innate goodness. That is why my grid for doing Step Four includes a third column under the heading Qualities. Healing is happening even as we struggle through our inventory, for we are growing in honesty, humility and courage, as well as many other qualities, such as the seven virtues of faith, hope, charity, justice, fortitude, temperance and prudence. Pointing out this personal growth for persons doing Step Five can be very encouraging to those facing the daunting challenge of this personal moral inventory. We don't need, nor do we deserve, to beat ourselves up to create an inventory. We just need to be faithful to the truth.

Moral inventory: Mining for Gold!

Wrongdoing	Defects	Qualities
Theft ←	Greed	Honesty
Adultery ←	Lust	Humility
Drunk ←	Grief	Faith
Sexual Abuse ←	Power	Love
Gossip ←	Jealousy	Courage
Fighting ←	Anger	Compassion
Neglect ←	Selfishness	Hope
Lying ←	Fear	Patience
		Forgiveness
(Sin) Words, Actions, Omissions, Thoughts	**(Sinfulness)** Painful emotions and Negative attitudes	
Steps 4 & 5 **Forgiveness**	**Steps 6 & 7** **Healing**	

Illustration 17

Our inventory invites us to look at all of our life story, the good, the bad and the ugly. A statement in one particular Step Four inventory guide states, "What we swore we would take to our graves and tell no one, tell it now." It is a searching and fearless moral inventory.

Our review of life begins with life in the womb. If our parents are still alive, we can ask them what was happening in their lives from our conception to birth. More and more scientific studies agree that we were being influenced by our parents' moods, feelings, spoken words, thoughts and the events that occurred while we were in the womb. These experiences are all part of us.

At one stage of my healing journey, I became aware that I was conceived in August, just before harvest, and born in April, just before spring seeding: both times can be extremely intense in the life of a farm family. I wrote earlier about my father's propensity to be a workaholic who almost never took a holiday. One can imagine the normal household and farming busyness compounded by these times of stress for very good people. I am sure that my entrance into the world in April at such a stressful time, when my father was too busy to notice my birth, was part of my recollected display when he declined to come in from the field on the day I had travelled so far to visit him.

I return to that example to underline the value of beginning Step Four with a focus on the time from conception, making that part of our examination of our childhood. Moving forward, then, we go from birth to the age when we began to remember. What was happening in our families during those crucial years? Was there tension, violence, addiction, lack of love, abandonment, even abuse?

If we have trouble remembering our childhood, is it because we have blocked out the painful memories? Our life is like an onion. We peel off what we can remember. That process may allow deeper layers to surface at another time.

Our memories will often be hurtful. We can then start looking at the way we reacted to the hurt in negative and hurtful ways, because we did not know how to deal with the memories or handle our pain. As a result, we acted out of our pain, and hurt others in the process. This is the more central focus of a Step Four, the actions for which we can and must take responsibility if we are to heal. At the same time, those reactions to our hurt cannot really be separated from the hurtful events that happened to us and from the character defects that resulted from that hurt. This will be discussed and described in more detail in Steps Six and Seven.

The primary focus of Step Four is the wrongdoing. The sample list in *Illustration 17* shows that our destructive behaviour consists of specific actions, words or omissions, such as neglect. These are the ways that we acted out of our painful emotions, how we survived and protected ourselves in destructive ways from further hurt, how we simply reacted to hurt by hurting others in turn. We name this *sin* or *wrongdoing*. We must stop denying and blaming and must take responsibility for what we have done to hurt others. We can change neither the past, nor the people, nor their perceptions of how we hurt them. But we can choose to change how we deal with the past and how we respond to the hurt in our lives. This is what Step Four is all about.

Step Four includes looking ahead to Step Six, in that sin and wrongdoing do not come from a vacuum. Most of our Step Four wrongdoing is a reaction to the lack of love and very real hurt that we have experienced in our life, physically, mentally, emotionally, sexually and spiritually. This hurt caused deep painful emotions and negative attitudes within us. We name these *sinfulness* (that which makes us sin) or *defects of character*. These emotions and attitudes are the root of our hurtful behaviour, as shown by the second column in the grid in *Illustration 17*. It is good to start noting these as we proceed through our Step Four inventory, for this will lead us into the work of Step Six and Seven.

Completing Step Four adds another image to our understanding of God or Higher Power in Step Three, the image of God as a garbage collector. God does not want our perfection but desires our weakness, brokenness, wrongdoing and sin. God's strength is at its best in our weakness (2 Corinthians 12:9). All we need do in this step is to be humble and totally honest in admitting all our wrongdoing, sin and garbage, and give it all to God in a sincere Step Five.

Step Four involves a healthy sense of guilt and an honest sense of shame, not false guilt and imposed shame. Working this step can give us the permission we need to name and deal with our own guilt and shame.

A key aspect of a healing spirituality is transformation, change and movement from darkness into the light. For years, many of us have denied, blamed, avoided, numbed out, minimized and escaped the painful emotions of confronting and acknowledging our negative, dysfunctional pasts. Step Four invites us to change, to *metanoia*, to turn around, to stop running away or escaping, and asks us to deal with our past, our dark reality. This step gently and firmly invites us to focus on ourselves for a change. We can't change others, but we can work on ourselves and open ourselves up to the possibility of change. We are invited to "befriend our shadow," as John Monbourquette put it in his book by that title. One way to befriend our shadow is to share that shadow with a trusted other, which is what happens in Step Five.

STEP FIVE: Trust

Admitted to God, to ourselves, and to another human being the exact nature of our wrongs.

So confess your sins to one another,
and pray for one another to be cured;
the heartfelt prayer of someone upright
works very powerfully. (James 5:16)

*

A farmer once confessed that he had stolen some hay. When asked by the priest how much hay he had stolen, he replied that he didn't know, as he was getting the rest that night!

This is not the way to celebrate Step Five. Step Five is a major overhaul of our way of life – a freeing of ourselves from the burden of the past and especially from guilt and fear, and doing so with rigorous honesty. There is a saying: *Name it; claim it; don't blame it; tame it and then aim it.* If we deal with our painful dark reality, it will be transformed and become something sacred that will empower us to help others as we share with them our experience in Step Twelve. It is here that we really begin to experience the love of God as trust and acceptance that set us free from guilt and fear.

Doing a Step Five

In Step Four, we admitted to God and to ourselves the exact nature of our wrongs. This is a first step in forgiving ourselves. By doing so, we admit our actions and accept ourselves as struggling, growing and healing human beings. Acknowledging that we are not bad people but rather good people who have done some bad things is the start of self-forgiveness.

Now we are asked to grow in love and trust and to share our deepest, darkest secrets with another human being. Many balk at this, asking why they cannot simply confess all this to God. The simplest answer is that this is how God wants it and how God works best. This confession is not so much to God as to another human being. We are humans, and until we can trust another human being, we may be kidding ourselves that we trust God. Do we want to tell our story to God and trust only God because God doesn't talk back?

A saying I found in my father's bible after he died surprised me: "To be closer to God, be closer to people." How true. The reality of the Incarnation, that the Son of God became one of us and took on our flesh, proclaims loudly that there is something holy about being human and fully living out our humanity.

Step Five is a beautiful way to experience the love, forgiveness and acceptance of God through another human being. This love heals us. According to John Monbourquette, the famed psychologist Carl Jung reminds us that "those who cannot unveil their conscience to another are destined to 'spiritual isolation.'"[39] Spiritual isolation results from lack of trust.

Carey Landry, a liturgist, wrote the hymn "Lay Your Hands." One of the lines is "Lord, we come to you through one another." He is right. We experience God best through one another, and particularly when we are in need.

Another reason for doing Step Five is the power of storytelling. There is a growing mountain of evidence among behaviourists and clergy that storytelling has therapeutic power. This step entails telling my story to someone else. The more I describe the details of what I have done, the more I will feel the emotions involved, and the more those emotions will heal and be salved.

Step Five is also a graced moment of intimacy, belonging and acceptance. To share my deepest secrets with another human being is a profound experience of intimacy, and this is love. Many persons yearn for intimacy, yet are terrified of it. This step is a safe way to experience that life-giving intimacy in a way many people are unable to do. This also addresses our deep human need for belonging and acceptance. To be heard and understood by another is to experience a deep sense of belonging and acceptance that is all about love, a love that heals and gives life.

At a Marriage Encounter team training weekend, a participant was trying to answer the question "How do I feel when I achieve intimacy with my spouse?" She said that it felt like there were no boundaries, barriers or obstacles between them. Listening to her, I realized that she was talking about salvation. She was already experiencing the eternal life that awaits us in heaven, in her present intimate relationship with her husband.

The words of John 14:21 led me to this conclusion. Jesus states, "They who have my commandments and keep them are those who love me; and those who love me will be loved by my Father, and I will love them and *reveal myself to them.*"

It is that simple. In Step Three, we saw God as love, unity, trust and intimate relationship. It is this same Trinitarian God whom we experience, who is revealed to us within an intimate, trusting relationship. In this light, the statement in my father's bible, quoted above, makes sense. This closeness or trust extends to admitting sin and wrongdoing to another in order to experience God's understanding, forgiveness and God's love, and that is what Step Five is all about.

One morning at 2:30, I received a call from the wife of an A.A. member. She said her husband was extremely agitated and unable to sleep, even though he had been given sleeping pills and anti-depression medication to help him. She asked if I would see him, and I agreed. He came to the rectory, and presented as depressed and suicidal.

I asked how he, as an A.A. member, was working the steps. He shared that 13 years earlier, he had superficially done Steps Four and Five, but had not revealed all, due to his fear and lack of trust. Now, years later, he was depressed, and sick and tired of living.

We talked about the need for humility, rigorous honesty, trust and the fearless and searching nature of Step Four. My impression was that of a man who had gone from Step One to Step Twelve without working honestly the steps in between. I shared that with him. It seemed to move him, as he broke down and cried. He then summoned up the courage to disclose what he had been carrying for so many years, and did a sincere Step Five. He left around 5:30 a.m., a free man. He has since shared this story at A.A. meetings and Roundups. There is great power in a sincere Step Five.

Receiving a Step Five

This is an appropriate place to include a way of receiving a Step Five. I have found the following grid very helpful as a way of both guiding others through a Step Five and also preparing them to move on to Steps Six to Nine. Although quite similar to the moral inventory illustration of Step Four, it is focused more precisely on facilitating the process of receiving a Step Five. The contents of the grid serve only as examples.

The grid shows graphically that most, if not all, of our acting out and wrongdoing flows from the anger, resentment and a host of other emotions and character defects in the second column. These painful emotions and character defects have their source in the hurt, trauma or lack of love in our lives. This is the material that we will take into Steps Six and Seven for healing. We also take into Steps Six and Seven the list of resentments towards those who have hurt us in one way or the other, so Resentments merits a column of its own.

A Grid for Receiving a Step Five

Wrongdoing	Character Defects	Resentments	Qualities
Lying Theft Gossip Adultery Neglect Drunkenness Stoned Murder Fighting Sexual abuse Etc. *Specific Actions Words, Thoughts or Omissions* Steps 4 & 5, 8 & 9	Guilt Greed Insecurity Lust Selfishness Loneliness Low esteem Hatred Resentment Need for power False pride Stubbornness Impatience Etc. *Painful Feelings Negative Attitudes* Steps 6 & 7	Parents Boss Siblings Abusers False friends Spouse Partner Children Etc. *Learning to Forgive* Steps 6 & 7	Humility Honesty Courage Love Forgiveness Acceptance Dignity Etc.
Losses	**Amends**	**Roots of Addiction**	**Addictions**
Childhood Language Culture Family Education Livelihood Marriage Relationship Etc. *Coming to Acceptance* Steps 6 & 7	Parents Children Siblings Employer Co-workers Friends Relatives Etc. *Learning to Apologize* Steps 8 & 9	Abandonment Lack of love Trauma Sexual Abuse Etc.	Alcohol Drugs Work Food Sex Gambling Etc.

In the section on Steps Six and Seven, we will see that the second part of doing Step Six is dealing with the grief and loss that are associated with the hurt that comes our way. For that reason, I included a column of the losses that one who is doing Step Five may reveal, even if he or she is not aware of those losses. Pointing out the need to recover from these losses will help the person move on to Steps Six and Seven. Another column that I find helpful is a list of those to whom a person needs to make amends that surfaces as they are telling their story, especially for the wrongdoing through which they have hurt others. This, too, helps them to move on to Steps Eight and Nine.

The last two columns can facilitate the participant's movement towards more lasting sobriety by providing greater awareness into their addictions, as well as the root of those addictions. There may be some surprises here that will help the individual with Steps Ten to Twelve when it is time to take those Steps.

Now, it is time to explore the program's core. Perhaps the least understood yet most powerful parts of the Twelve Step program are Steps Six and Seven.

STEP SIX: Forgiveness

*Were entirely ready to have God remove
all these defects of character.*

"If your brother does something wrong,
go and have it out with him alone, between your two selves.
If he listens to you, you have won back your brother.
If he does not listen to you, take one or
two others along with you:
whatever the misdemeanour, the evidence of
two or three witnesses
is required to sustain a charge." (Matthew 18:15-17)

*

The very heart of the Twelve Step program rests in Steps Six and Seven. Working these two steps earnestly is the key to the transforming power of the Twelve Steps that are centred on the ability to forgive hurt and accept loss.

In Part Three, we spoke of the fight, flight or freeze mentality we experience when we feel afraid, terrified or under attack. The fight or flight response is exactly that – fighting or fleeing the threat; the freeze response, something common to victims of sexual abuse, happens when one attempts to become invisible to a potential abuser.

The Fourth Way of Forgiveness

There is, however, a fourth option that comes to us from Steps Six and Seven. This option is open to us if we are faith-based persons. The option is to forgive. The steps, worked properly, *move us towards forgiveness*, as indicated in the following chart. They are made easier to remember because every word starts with the letter "F".

Fight – (Fury)
Flight – (Fear)
Freeze – (Terror)
Forgive – (Faith)

Note the emphasis on the words *move us towards forgiveness*. It is essential to clarify what forgiveness is at the outset of this step. For too many people, forgiveness is a "million miles away," as one person put it. For others, even the use of the word sounds repugnant. Some authors speak only of forgiving one's self, and leave it at that.

At a 2007 Truth and Reconciliation conference in Calgary, Alberta, convened by then Assembly of First Nations Chief Phil Fontaine, I gave a presentation in which I mentioned the need to move towards forgiveness. A psychologist present aggressively chastised me for using the word "forgiveness." She claimed that this word did not belong in the process, that I should never have mentioned this word, that I was only using it because I was a Christian.

I replied that, based on my experience over many years, unless victims at least start to move towards forgiveness, they would remain angry for the rest of their lives. Her retort was that it was okay to be angry as long as it did not control a person. The conversation ended civilly, but I learned how deeply convinced some people are that forgiveness is an impossible pipe dream and not a factor in their approach to healing. This saddened me, and I felt sorry for the victims who would be cheated of the opportunity to experience freedom from anger and resentment if they shared that narrow, dead-end view.

At this point, I want to include an example of what this lack of forgiveness can lead to. Some years ago, a group of penal psychologists gave a presentation at a wellness conference. As part of their presentation, they handed out a letter written by a 15-year-old girl to her imprisoned father. No explanation for sharing that letter was given. Perhaps they simply ran out of time.

I was both shocked at the nature of the letter and grateful that we had been given a copy. This letter graphically illustrated the invisible prison that the one who refuses to forgive ends up living in. The letter is presented below as it was given to us.

Dad,

I don't know what to say to you, other than the fact that I hate you with all my heart. Why would you do something like that to me? You always said you would never hurt us kids, but you did. You did things to me that I can never forgive you for. Why me, you bastard? I hate you so much, my own dad. You treated us like crap and didn't seem to care. You would treat our mother like shit. But we still all loved you. Why me, Dad? Why and how could you do this to me? I trusted and loved you. You hurt me so much that I'll never know how to trust someone again. I'm scared of you. What you did was sick. What did I do to deserve this pain you have caused me? Your letter to me was shit. I don't care if you have problems. Look what you have caused me. I don't care about anything anymore. Why should I? You touched me in ways a father is not supposed to. You sick bastard. Every time I think of it I get sick. I want you to die for all this. You can rot in hell. I hope while you are in jail you are hurt in many ways. You are my father but I don't have one anymore. You destroyed that. Are you happy that you did this to me? Are you happy that you will never see me or your grandkids ever? I am very happy that you are out of my life. I hate myself for all the shit I let you do.

What was it that made you pick me and not the others? Was I stupid or ugly – why, why, why? I hate you. Nothing you can ever say will make me your daughter again. You stopped having me as a daughter when you did those sick things to me, and what you made me do. I was scared and very afraid to talk to anyone about this. I thought nobody would believe me. I was right. "You couldn't do that," is what everyone said. But you did. You lied to everyone. Now they know and you will never hurt me again. You are dead to me and I can only hope that nobody else ever has to go through what I did. You will always be in my mind as a bastard.

I sometimes try and think of the good times. But I can't get over the fact that you did sexual things to me. Did it make you feel like a man? You are a dog and not a man. I can't stand to even think of you. Stay out of my life and don't try to talk to me either, you pig. I wish you were never my father then this wouldn't have happened to me. Why me, dad? Why me? I can't think of what I did to be treated like this. You mustn't have loved me at all. Did I do something to make you treat me in this way? What was it? Tell me. What was going on with your mind? Are you crazy or just totally sick? I don't want you to call, write or ever see me again. So don't answer these questions to me. It just makes me feel better to write them out. I want nothing to do with you ever again.

PS: May your life be a total hell and may you never be happy again. You made mine a hell and I can only hope to be happy one day. Rot in hell, you pig. I am no longer your daughter.

How can one feel anything but profound sadness after reading a letter like this? I fear that these psychologists thought that this girl had done good work in venting her anger and expressing it towards her father, without taking her any further. My fear is that she will remain in that prison of anger for the rest of her life. The limited stance of the psychologists, and her stubborn refusal to consider any other option, will shut down and cut off any hope of forgiveness, healing and reconciliation for both this girl and her father. Such is the negative impact of un-forgiveness.

Müller-Fahrenholz states,

> The act of forgiveness begins with a decision to no longer be controlled by the effects of past wrongdoing as well as a choice for a different kind of future. In the acceptance of the apology, the victim converts it into a gift that is reciprocated by the gift of forgiveness. This gift exchange results in the unlocking of a painful bondage of past wrongdoing, resulting in liberation for both victims and oppressors. Depending on the extent of the wrongdoing, forgiveness can present a challenge of staggering proportions.[40]

This is the challenge facing this young girl. Unfortunately, it appears she has no one to walk with her through this journey.

I believe that if we are to be free from carrying anger and resentment, forgiveness is a must. However, forgiveness must also be understood, so that it is less of a stumbling block for us to grant forgiveness to others.

Forgiveness is a process that occurs over time. It is okay if we cannot yet find it in our hearts to forgive or even to think of forgiveness at the present. We simply need to be open to the possibility in the future.

Forgiveness can also be transformative, as was my experience recounted in the opening Case Study. It can happen in an instant, all at once, a sudden shift in which emotions and attitudes can suddenly take on a whole new light, opening up the possibility of creating an entirely new future for ourselves and others as well.

Daniel O'Leary writes in a delicate, poetic way about this possibility of a new future open to those who can forgive. His gentle insights encourage us to explore this challenging world of forgiveness:

> There are two such inner spaces for grace that I am learning to treasure. One has to do with the tiny but eternal space we

make room for, when we hold off, even for a split second, the negative – even violent – reaction to a sudden hurt, allowing into our souls a sliver of saving light. In that tiny oasis we recover our almost-lost balance and center, our precarious peace. It lasts the space of a breath – but hides heaven.[41]

Forgiveness as a Process

To begin the process of forgiveness, one must accept the hurt that has been done to us. We can start "forgiving the event" by admitting that it happened, that it was real, that someone or something did hurt us at a very deep level. We can choose to let go of denial and avoidance, and become willing to deal with the reality of that hurt.

Next we can move on to letting go of the desire for revenge, to even the score. Exacting revenge may give the illusion of satisfaction, but it simply adds more violence and guilt to the world. Good spirituality is about letting go. Here we can practise good spirituality by letting go of our desire for revenge. In doing so, we let go of brooding over, thinking about and embellishing the hurtful event.

It is striking that the three behavioural stances that psychologists speak about (aggression, passivity, or assertiveness) coincide precisely with the four options outlined earlier (fight, flight, freeze, or forgive).

The process of forgiveness/assertiveness may eventually lead us to forgive the person who hurt us in the first place. Forgiveness at this stage can be a breakthrough for those who understand forgiveness, or it can be an obstacle for those who don't. It is important, therefore, to explore even more deeply this mystery of forgiveness.

The Essence of Forgiveness

I am indebted here to Ronald Rolheiser for his valuable and penetrating insight into the nature of forgiveness, based on the biblical connotation of the word "pondering." In this sense, to forgive is to "ponder" – to hold, carry and transform tension, i.e., to not give back in kind – anger for anger, hate for hate, bitterness for bitterness, but to transform hate to love, bitterness to graciousness, and hurt into forgiveness.

The biblical model for this, of course, is Jesus. On the cross, Jesus was taking in all the negative energy of those who abused him and were killing him, and transformed it into forgiveness. The good news is that when we do the same, when we act like God and forgive, we get to feel like God. I am convinced that Jesus on the cross, while in terrible pain, was at peace, because he knew he was doing the Father's will. So it is with us when, empowered by the Spirit, we forgive those who have hurt us in any way. This negative energy transformed by our Higher Power into the energy of love is the essence of forgiveness, and this forgiveness and healing are the foundations of Steps Six and Seven.

For many people, completion of Step Five seems to be understood as a graduation, an indication that they have arrived and completed their work. This often occurs as they leave a treatment centre. They seem to lack clarity as to how to move on in the program to the next steps and continued healing. From my experience over the years of listening to people sharing their Step Five, I have developed a guide to provide that greater clarity and to help them move on to working Steps Six and Seven.

Step Six Guide: *Forgiveness and Healing*

*Were entirely ready to have God remove
all these defects of character.*

STAGE ONE: *DEAL WITH THE HURT*
(Going beyond anger, resentment and blame)

A. Remember the events; relive the experience.

B. Feel the emotions and stay with the emotions, especially the anger, hurt, pain.

C. Express the emotions in a positive way.

– Anger therapy

– Vigorous exercise, etc.

– Share them with others, at meetings, or one-on-one

- Communicate with love directly or by letter or phone, using the formula:

   1. Ask their permission to share personally.

   2. "When you ..." (describe the behaviour of the other).

   3. "I feel/felt ..." (describe your feelings).

Note: Remember to keep it clean. No revenge, punishment or blame: "To confront with expectation is manipulation."

D. Try to understand the other.

E. Tell your inner child, "It's not your fault."

F. Pray sincerely for the one who hurt you, what you would want for yourself.

G. Thank God for each abuser, for God's love has turned evil to good by healing you and empowering you to love as God loves – you have changed!

STAGE TWO: *GRIEVING THE LOSS*
(Going beyond sadness, grief and self-pity)

A. Remember the events; relive the experiences.

B. Identify and name your losses.

C. Feel and stay with the emotions, especially sadness and self-pity.

D. Express the emotions positively:

   – Share the feelings with a friend or group. (Grief shared is grief diminished.)

   – Write a letter with love expressing feelings towards the deceased and read it out loud.

E. Mourn and grieve the losses.

F. Give yourself permission to cry as much as you need to.

G. Take a workshop on grieving.

H. Say the words "It's gone, it's gone."

Briefly, let us explore this guide and unpack it. The first thing to note is that it is made up of two parts: first, dealing with anger, and then dealing with loss. Whenever there is a painful hurt in our lives, invariably this is accompanied by some kind of loss, and both need to be addressed. Let's look first at Stage One.

Stage One: Dealing with Anger

A. Remember the events; relive the experience.

We try to avoid pain, and we block out memories by trying to forget painful experiences. We need to turn that around and give ourselves permission to remember, to think, to relive those painful events. As we learned earlier, the emotions may hurt intensely, but they will not harm us. It is repressing our emotions that can lead us to do harm to ourselves and to others.

B. Feel the emotions and stay with the emotions, especially the anger, hurt, pain.

Once the emotions start surfacing, our instinct once again is to run from the pain, to medicate the pain through addictive activity. We need to give ourselves permission to feel the pain, to be human once again, to be real and to feel our emotions.

C. Express the feelings in a positive way.

We need to validate rather than repress our emotions by acknowledging them, naming them and, above all, by expressing them in a positive way. We need to empty ourselves of these painful emotions by giving them away. Doing anger therapy can be helpful (preferably in a nonviolent way). Vigorous exercise is also helpful. Above all, sharing those emotions with others at meetings or one on one leads to healing.

What I have found to be most effective is what I call *Communicating with Love*. In various forms, this is a method used by some rehabilitation centres, especially those that have a family week where families and clients take turns confronting each other.

This is based on Matthew 18:15, where Jesus tells his disciples how to forgive (the quote that began this section). There are three stages to forgiving:

1. It is helpful to ask permission to share something with the person personally.
2. Then describe the hurtful behaviour of the person, what actually happened between the two of you. (This will not be a surprise, but will serve only as a reminder to the person.)
3. Then add how you felt, and perhaps still feel, about those actions and how they impacted your life.

It is important to stop there, at the period, and not add any expectation, revenge or name calling, no matter how much you might feel like doing this. The love is in the discipline of describing the event, sharing the feelings and letting go of the desire for revenge and for getting even. It is here that good spirituality becomes letting go, because to confront with expectation is manipulation, not love. It is also here that love truly becomes a decision, far beyond emotions and feelings. Love as a decision is also the key to letting go, to forgiving and moving on.

It is best to *communicate with love* in person or by sending a letter. However, when this is not possible or advisable, much healing can still take place by reading a letter out loud to a pillow or to a trusted other, doing a ritual burning of the letter, and sharing that experience with others, respecting confidentiality, if needed.

D. Try to **understand** the other.

When we are able to enter into the psyche of the other person, to feel their feelings and understand where they are coming from, forgiveness becomes a lot easier.

Tom shared how he was able to let go of his anger towards an uncle who physically abused him when he was younger. One day he learned that his uncle was also abused as a young boy. Later in life after a car accident, his uncle was left in a very stressful life situation that saw him also caring for his brother's children. That awareness was enough for Tom to let go of all anger towards his uncle, to forgive him and to move on with his life with a degree of peace. Recall also how my understanding of my father's feelings led to my ability to forgive him, as I did my Steps Six and Seven with him in mind.

E. Tell your inner child, "It's not your fault."

Often, those who are hurt revictimize themselves by taking on false guilt and blaming themselves, especially when the abuser was a trusted and loved family member. We may need to let go of that false guilt, and tell ourselves over and over that it was not our fault.

F. For the one who hurt you, pray sincerely for what you would want for yourself.

This is certainly not easy, but it is very effective. This is where Christian spirituality shines forth strongly as a way of "loving our enemy" and "doing good to those who persecute us." Prayer is necessary, because for the most part, this is beyond us without God's grace and power. We may need to "faith it until we make it."

G. Thank God for each abuser.

God's love has turned evil to good by healing you and empowering you to love as God loves. You have changed. This also may seem impossible, but it is a great discipline to practise as we try to move towards forgiveness.

I experienced this during a 10-day silent retreat at the Franciscan St. Michael's Retreat House in Lumsden, nestled in the Qu'Appelle Valley of southern Saskatchewan. For whatever reason, one day during that retreat, I found myself thanking God for each hurtful person and event in my life, for each loss I had encountered and each goal that had not materialized. I was taken by surprise by this almost subconscious development. I took this awareness to my spiritual director. She reflected that my healing had come full circle now that I was able to thank God and be grateful for both the hurtful, as well as the pleasant, events of my life.

Recall the painful letter written by a young girl who was unable even to consider forgiving her father. She was probably counselled to think that this was an appropriate response to her deep hurt. By contrast, I would like now to share with you an amazing letter of forgiveness.

The writer was a client for the 14th time at a rehabilitation centre. I asked him if he had any experience of working the Twelve Steps. He replied that at previous centres, he had been given some papers and information and told to work them, but really had no idea how to go about doing this. I assured him that during our sessions, we would be doing a thorough journey through the Twelve Steps. I encouraged him to take them seriously and to work them during his stay.

Just before his marbling-out ceremony and departure some weeks later, I dropped by to see how he was doing and to say goodbye. To my delight, he had spent the last week at the centre writing a dozen letters to those he had hurt (Step Nine) and to those who had hurt him (Step Six). He wanted me to read them all. I declined due to time constraints, and said I would read one.

I took a copy of the letter he offered me. When I read it later, I could not hold back my tears of joy and gratitude. That letter was to his mother. In it, he was doing his best to forgive her for the pain and hurt she had caused him all the years of his life. This letter is a poignant masterpiece of Step Six forgiveness and grief work. It filled me with deep hope for him and for anyone who chooses to sincerely work these steps. The letter speaks for itself. It is long, so I will include only key portions that serve as a model of healing possibilities for one who is dealing with life's hurts in the context of the Twelve Step program.

My dear mom,

> You have put me through a lot. I feel old. I want to start off with issues that I have with you as a child. From the first time I can remember I have never heard you say, "I love you." You never carried me or hugged me. For the longest time I have been asking myself, "Do you really love me?" I really don't know still. Are you just going through the motions and doing things because you are my biological mother or do you really

love me? I felt abandoned by you, emotionally neglected as a child. In a lot of ways I felt unloved. A lot of times I felt like I didn't belong in this world. I longed for a hug and didn't get it. I never felt validated. I don't remember one positive word. Was I a good boy? Was I handsome? Was I strong? Was I smart, and were you proud of me?

Before I turned 12 I felt like I was garbage and saw the world as a scary place where I didn't belong. I didn't feel your love. I was angry, hurting and felt rejected. My first drink to ease the pain was when you came home after you and B. had gone for 3-4 days and got home on my birthday. You had promised me a stick and skates. You were both drinking but not drunk. I asked you for the skates because this was my special day and I thought you might feel guilty for being gone for so long. You yelled at me and told me to get out of here, there was no skates; there was nothing for my birthday. I was devastated, hurt and angry. I felt rejected, unloved. I didn't matter, what my grandparents were telling me all along was right – you didn't love me. I lost my soul that night. I was a worthless human being nobody cared about. I was deeply wounded. I felt like crying but I was empty. I couldn't cry. I was detached from my body and I was angry and full of hate. The seven beers I stole off you and B. took me away to another reality, one that didn't hurt. I was floating on air and it felt so good to drink. I was running away from reality. With the realization that you didn't love me, I didn't give a F- about the world.

I became like a robot, I didn't know how to think, what to think, how to solve my own problems. I lost my ability to reason, I lost my ability to have sound judgment, to care about anyone, or anything; I didn't know how to feel. I was in a dark cloud and I couldn't see anything but darkness and negativity. I felt like I was crazy. I felt sorry for myself. I was full of hate and rage. I was ashamed of myself; I hated what I was, whoever I was and I couldn't stand to be in my own skin. Nobody cared; everybody was out to get me. I was having paranoid delusions. I was detached from reality and prayed to God for help, to stop the abuse, the deep pain. I felt everybody had abandoned me including you by your actions. God didn't want to help me either. I questioned why I was on earth, for what purpose and I wanted to end it all at age 13. I was going to shoot myself. I rejected God and cursed Him and said I would follow the dark force. I put the gun to my face but I couldn't pull the trigger. The reason was that I had to find out if my mom ever loved me. I couldn't leave this world without finding out. I couldn't give my abusers the satisfaction. Although I felt like you hated me, I still loved you and I couldn't embarrass you by killing myself. Still at this time some of the things you did to me further cemented the belief that you didn't love me, that you were ashamed of me, and that you thought I was a worthless human being. I hated you. I was very angry and deeply hurt. At one time you even made fun of me. At a time when I needed understanding, you laughed in my face. You played emotional and psychological games with me. I feel like you did that intentionally. You kept wounding me more.

Then suddenly I was an adult. I was in jail for the first time in the city. I hated you and the world. I was very slowly finding about the world. I still hated who I was, nothing changed, but now I was a criminal, not just a drunk. I had no respect for myself, for anyone. I started to suffer from panic attacks and severe anxiety attacks. I was scared of people, couldn't look anyone in the eye. I was scared of crowds. I lived like a hermit, a recluse, an alcoholic, a self-conscious wounded person who didn't know how to heal. I was still a little child.

Comes R. and I slowly started my healing journey. For that I thank her. The prior treatment centers didn't do anything because I wasn't ready. I am still slowly learning to heal, learning about my sickness. I am ready to let go of my garbage, my shame, my resentments, and let go of all the anger and pain. I now know I am a loveable person as God intended for me to be.

I want to be free of all this. I need to know if you love me. You must tell me. I must hear it. I forgive you for all that you put me through, for all the pain that you intentionally caused me, for all the hurtful things you said and did. I shall never know why you did them but as a child and a human being I didn't deserve it.

By sharing more of my story with people and circles I am gaining back my childhood kid and know it was not his fault. The hold my pain and hurt has on me lessens the more I talk and share it. Mom, I forgive you. I wish I had more answers but I won't force you to talk. I hope you can heal too. Deal with your demons. As human beings shame kills us spiritually and emotionally. I will pray for you. I don't blame you.

With love, your son, R.

This man had successfully followed the guidelines for doing Step Six. He remembered the painful events, felt the emotions, stayed with the emotions, and then shared those emotions with his mother with love, not once acting out of anger. He chose to share his feelings of anger and pain with his mother as a way of freeing himself from the hold they had on him and as a way of moving towards forgiving his mother. This is an example of truly working Step Six and opening all kinds of doors and opportunities for healing and reconciliation.

Sometimes the person that we have to forgive is ourselves. We can be harder on ourselves than on anyone else. Remember that the third part of the Great Commandment is to love ourselves.

I remember an Easter when I was obsessively berating and punishing myself for resigning a position with the Oblates. A friend said to me that as far as he was concerned, my refusal to forgive myself was worse than anything else I had ever done. I was taken aback. I didn't think I could ever forgive myself. He went on to tell me that during the exchange of peace at the Vigil that night, he was going to say to me, "He is risen, alleluia!" and that he wanted me to repeat it back to him.

My memory of that Vigil is vivid. As I listened to the readings and the homily, my stubborn, self-condemning attitude started to crack and my emotions shifted. When my friend came up to me at the exchange of peace, I responded sincerely, "He is risen, alleluia," and I actually felt hope, release and new life pouring into me. That night, I was able to play the guitar and sing for the first time in many months. I had started to forgive myself.

With this reflection on Stage One, dealing with anger, let us now take a closer look at Stage Two, dealing with grief and loss.

Stage Two: Dealing with Grief and Loss

As we enter into this portion of the Step Six guide, it is good to remind ourselves that every hurt carries with it a loss of some kind. Something has changed that will never be recovered and that must be grieved, as hurt that is not grieved will often come back as hardness and depression. We explore now the process of grieving.

A. Remember the events; relive the experiences.

As in dealing with hurt and anger, we are invited once again to stop fleeing our pain by medicating it in some way and to do just the opposite with faith, namely, to remember the events and to go through the pain. Remember, the only way through the pain is through the pain.

B. Identify and name your losses.

The more specific our recall of events, the more the emotions and feelings will return, and the more likely it will be that healing will happen. We are invited to identify and name our losses and the persons who were involved in those losses, as a way of dealing with the reality of that loss.

C. Feel and stay with the emotions, especially sadness and self-pity.

The pain involved in the healing process is the pain of feeling the emotions that we stuffed and repressed for so many years. We are invited to name, validate and honour our emotions by feeling them and staying with them, and in the process, to become more fully human.

D. Express the emotions positively.

Again, it is important to transform our painful emotions. We can share the feelings with a friend, a trusted other or a group. We can write a letter expressing feelings towards a deceased person and read it out loud to a pillow or to someone else. Again, grief shared is grief diminished. We can also go to the cemetery and read our letter at the gravesite of our loved one or the person who hurt us. Rather than staying stuck in our grief, we can turn that grief into good, healthy grieving.

E. Mourn and grieve the losses.

As uncomfortable as this may feel, it is important to do this. This is especially difficult for men, but can be critical for them. It is this reservoir of painful emotions that emerges so often when men are under the influence of alcohol or drugs. The inhibitions are lessened and those repressed emotions begin to surface in an unhealthy way. We need to give ourselves permission to mourn and to grieve our losses in a healthy way, and healing will happen.

F. Give yourself permission to cry.

Crying is an important part of the grieving process. We can give ourselves permission to cry as much as we need to. Sometimes, well-meaning people are too quick to offer solace that actually can hinder or block the grieving process. Parents who have lost a child will take longer than usual to let go of that pain, and they may need to cry for years. One may never really get over losing a spouse. Men have been socialized not to cry. Some men are afraid that, if they begin to cry, they may never stop. Again, it is good to recall that repressing our emotions and our tears can be another form of emotional abuse.

G. Take a workshop on grieving.

Thankfully, more and more workshops on grieving are being offered. I recall as a young Oblate missionary seeing an ad for a grief workshop at a local retreat centre, and wondering what that was all about. I was actually even a bit smug, thinking that I would never need this. How wrong I was, and how much I had to learn. Most of us can benefit from this help for our grieving process.

H. Say the words *"It's gone, it's gone."*

This can be a way of letting the reality of the loss sink in and become more real. These words can also be a way of letting go of the pain of the loss, of admitting to ourselves the reality of that loss.

I had a powerful experience of grieving during a four-day fast, linked to the experience of self-forgiveness mentioned earlier. I had attended a congress of our Oblate province in which there was a discernment process for future leadership of our group. The question of leadership brought back painful memories of when I had resigned as provincial leader due to burnout. During this leadership review, my name did not surface at all. I was disappointed, and felt like I had lost the respect of my Oblate brothers. I left that congress sad and unsettled, the feeling that I took into the four-day fast.

One of the helpers at the fast happened to remark that the majority of people in treatment centres are struggling with unresolved grief issues. That phrase stuck in my mind and was very present to me as I sat by my hogan, tending the fire. When asked by the support elder how I was doing, I shared with him this thought of "unresolved grief issues" that was puzzling me. He advised me to just stay with it and be present to it.

Sometime later, I noticed that a log burning on the fire was starting to sizzle. I realized that it was a green log and had lots of moisture in it; the moisture would have to come out somewhere. The rings in the wood and two termite holes that looked like eyes made the end of the log look like a smiling face. Suddenly, sap started to pour out of the log from one of the termite holes. The image struck me like a thunderclap: the log was crying, and I needed to cry. I needed to grieve and to mourn.

I decided to do some grief work, no matter how uncomfortable I felt. There was an old car nearby, half hidden in the bush, and I found my way there. It was quite intact, so I sat inside and closed the door.

I then allowed myself to remember all the things that did not work out in my life: all my losses, starting with the loss of my French language in the hospital when I was five, followed by the loss of sporting events during my youth due to the work ethic at home, and then my unhappy years as a day scholar at college. Twice I quit university due to lack of clarity as to why I was there. In my third year, I had resigned as president of the student union for the same reason, losing the respect and esteem of my fellow students. That pattern repeated itself when I had to resign years later as provincial superior of our group of Oblates, the pain that was triggered by the recent congress.

The reality of these losses and the pain involved descended on me like a cloud. I began to cry, and pounded the steering wheel of the old car until my fists hurt. Then I pounded the seat, which immediately filled the old car with stale dust, so much so that I had to get out of the car. But when I emerged, I felt like a vacuum cleaner had sucked all that pain out of me. It stayed in the car. I was astounded to feel an amazing energy that filled me from head to toe. Suddenly, I realized that I had grieved. I had done some grief work, and the result was a freshness and vitality that was startling.

These two stages of Step Six, dealing with our hurt and anger by moving towards and learning to forgive, and dealing with our sadness and self-pity by allowing ourselves to grieve and mourn our losses, are powerful ways to experience the healing that is at the core of the Twelve Step program. As powerful as doing Step Six can be, remember that it goes hand in hand with Step Seven, and is only a precursor for Step Seven, a step that involves prayer and the work of our Higher Power.

STEP SEVEN: Healing

Humbly asked God to remove our shortcomings.
(and to fill us with the gifts of the Holy Spirit).

God will be gracious to you when your cry for help rings out;
As soon as he hears it, he will answer you.
Then the moonlight will be bright as sunlight
and sunlight itself be seven times brighter,
on the day Yahweh dresses his people's wound
and heals the scars of the blows they have received. (Isaiah 30:19b; 26b)

*

In Step Seven, we humbly ask God to do what we cannot do on our own – remove our defects of character so that we can truly be free. A profound experience of the healing power of this step happened to me while on retreat at the Immaculate Heart Retreat House in Spokane, just before being ordained a priest in 1974.

Upon arrival at the retreat house, we were invited to help out around the grounds. As I love gardening and even weeding, I was more than willing, so each day I would go out and weed a patch of garden. The second week that I was there, I noticed that the weeds were already starting to grow back, so I weeded the same patch of ground, a little deeper this time.

Towards the end of the third week, we experienced a healing Eucharist. The format was very simple. During the penitential rite, everyone had the opportunity to celebrate the Sacrament of Reconciliation (a mini Step Five). The priests heard each other's confession, and then those of the religious and laity. The Liturgy of the Word and Eucharist continued as usual, with a homily on the power of God to heal. Then, after the closing prayer, we were invited to come forward, share a particular need for healing, and receive the laying on of hands along with a healing prayer.

Though somewhat hesitant to do so, I felt challenged by that invitation to go a little deeper and deal with an issue in my life that was troubling me – my struggle at times with chastity, with my human sexuality and sexual energy. Adding urgency, and probably some courage, to this resolve was the fact that, in a few months, I would be ordained to the ministerial priesthood for life, and I did not want to carry this degree of struggle into my priesthood. So, mustering up all the honesty and courage I could, I went forward, articulated my need and received a simple healing prayer and laying on of hands. I didn't feel anything out of the ordinary, and left the experience at that.

The next day I went out to weed as usual. I noticed that the weeds were growing back a second time. With only one more week there, I resolved to do things differently. I would weed only a small part of the garden instead of the whole area, and would dig the weeds out by the roots.

I found a trowel and began to dig around the first weed. I was surprised at how deep I had to go to get to the bottom of it. As I was gently lifting it out, careful not to leave behind any miniscule tendrils that would grow back, I heard the words, not with my ears, but within my head, ringing distinctly and clearly, as if they were spoken by someone, "This is what I am doing to you on this retreat."

Startled, I looked around to see if there was anyone who might have spoken to me. There was no one in sight – I was alone. It dawned on me with awe that this was the answer to the healing prayer of the previous evening, a graced moment, a spiritual healing. Through the courage to be open and honest the evening before and that simple healing prayer, God was reaching deep within me to remove the character defect in question, taking it out by the root and filling me with purity, healing and serenity. And so it was – from that moment on, as the months and years went by, I was really free as never before from that tendency.

Years later, I realized that the healing I received that day was supported by the intimacy that I was able to maintain at that time of my life. And what a blessing that was for me. In a rather dramatic way, I had experienced Steps Four and Five, Six and Seven, forgiveness and healing, before I understood the program. And that power is available to all who "humbly ask God to remove their defects of character."

A prayer for Step Seven that the Big Book provides to help access this power is as follows: "My Creator, I am now willing that you should have all of me, good and bad. I pray that you now remove from me every single defect of character which stands in the way of my usefulness to you and my fellows. Grant me strength, as I go out from here, to do your bidding. Amen."[42]

You may be wondering about the addition to the heading of this section on Step Seven. As mentioned earlier, this is the only place in the program that seems incomplete from my spiritual perspective. That perspective teaches that the Son of God had a two-fold mission: to redeem and to sanctify, or in other words, to save (forgive) us and to heal us. This means that God does not so much pull our defects and sinfulness out of us, but rather fills us with the Spirit of Jesus.

That infilling of the Spirit transforms and heals us, leaving no room for the defects.

This view, being filled with God's healing grace, seems more positive than just being emptied of something negative. As a result, I added this dimension to Step Seven.

Someone who truly understands the subtle ways of God's grace working within the heart and mind of the human being is Reinhold Niebuhr, author of the Serenity Prayer so identified with the movement of A.A. His thoughtful and insightful reflection on faith, hope, love and forgiveness pulls together all that has been said in this book:

> Nothing that is worth doing can be achieved in our lifetime; therefore we must be saved by *hope*. Nothing which is true or beautiful or good makes complete sense in any immediate context of history; therefore we must be saved by *faith*. Nothing we do, however virtuous, can be accomplished alone; therefore we are saved by *love*. No virtuous act is quite as virtuous from the standpoint of our friend or foe as it is from our standpoint. Therefore we must be saved by the final form of love which is *forgiveness*.[43]

In one poignant paragraph, Niebuhr articulates the essence of this part of the Twelve Step program. With these thoughts in mind, let us now turn our attention to Steps Eight and Nine, steps that flow naturally from the experience of healing and learning to forgive in Steps Six and Seven, as well as the initial benefit of the forgiveness that we experience from Steps Four and Five.

STEP EIGHT: Courage

Made a list of all persons we had harmed,
and became willing to make amends to them all.

"Therefore, I tell you, her sins, which were many,
have been forgiven; hence she has shown great love.
But the one to whom little is forgiven, loves little."
(Luke 7:47)

*

In Step Five, we experienced forgiveness from God, ourselves and one other person. Now the program moves us into a broader experience of forgiveness from those we hurt when we were acting out of our addictions.

The most practical way to begin this step is to go back to the searching and fearless moral inventory we did in Step Four. There we painfully and humbly acknowledged all the harm we did by reacting to, coping with and surviving our original wounds of childhood and the hurt that came our way throughout our lives.

Now in Step Eight, we can begin to put names to the recipients of our hurtful reactive words, actions, thoughts or omissions. These are the unfortunate persons who crossed the path of our past vengeful manner of living.

Humble honesty, remorse, sorrow and contrition are the attitudes that we must cultivate and pray for here. What God wants of us is a humble spirit and a contrite heart. Here is where those virtues shine (Isaiah 57:15). We are asked to be humble and honest, to proceed with raw courage, to list all those we had harmed and to develop a genuine desire to make things right with them. This is what justice is all about: a right relationship with God, with others, with ourselves and with all of creation. This is a tall order, but it is what Steps Eight and Nine require, opening up the possibility of a deeper healing of relationships through reconciliation.

We need the courage of the woman in the scriptures mentioned above (Luke 7:36-50): having experienced the compassion, understanding and forgiveness of Jesus, she dared to enter the house of one of the leading Pharisees to make amends to Jesus by washing his feet with her tears and drying them with her hair, a gesture that has come down to us through the ages as an example to follow. As he mentions, she was showing great love, because she was forgiven much.

We are now arriving at the serenity of which both the program and the Serenity prayer speak. However, here we strive to go even deeper. We are building the reign of God, the Higher Power, among us.

As St. Paul writes in his letter to the Romans (Romans 14:17), the reign of God is not about eating or drinking, but rather the peace, the joy and the justice of the Holy Spirit. Peace is more than a passing feeling or fleeting emotion – it is a gift of the Holy Spirit. Joy is also much more than a passing feeling or fleeting emotion – it, too, is a gift of the Spirit. Justice is a right relationship, a life-giving and energizing relationship with our God, others, ourselves and all of God's creation. These three gifts are ours, and cannot be taken from us unless we choose to reject them. This is what we can hope to experience as we work these steps.

Step Eight, therefore, is not simply a filler or add-on to Step Nine. It is a profound prelude to and an important preparation for the deeper experience of forgiveness, healing and reconciliation that occurs within a genuine living out of Step Nine.

STEP NINE: Reconciliation

Made direct amends to such people wherever possible, except when to do so would injure them or others.

"So when you are offering your gift at the altar,
if you remember that your brother or sister
has something against you,
leave your gift at the altar and go;
first be reconciled with your brother or sister,
and then come and offer your gift." (Matthew 5:23-24)

*

Do you want to experience freedom and joy? Dare to ask for forgiveness. It is as simple as that.

Step Nine is the key to healing of relationships, and can therefore be a source of much joy. I use the word "can," because asking for forgiveness does not guarantee that reconciliation will happen. As Worthington and Drinkard assert, "Reconciliation is defined as the restoration of trust in an interpersonal relationship through mutual trustworthy behaviors.... Forgiveness is granted while reconciliation needs to be achieved."[44]

The person who commits an offence harms the relationship. The offender will probably feel guilt and fear, while the person who is harmed will probably feel hurt and anger. It is up to the wrongdoer to go to the other, admit wrongdoing, listen to the feelings of the hurting person and ask for forgiveness. If forgiveness is given, then reconciliation is possible. If that person is unable or not ready to forgive, then there is no reconciliation, but at least the one who apologizes is released from guilt and fear.

Listening to and truly hearing the pain of a person who is wronged are crucial elements of an apology by a wrongdoer. Compassion is the ability to feel deeply the pain of the other. The listening that we are called to here is exactly that – compassionate listening that seeks to feel the pain of the other, to experience it, to realize what we have put the other through by our hurtful actions. An apology can be a freely chosen powerlessness and vulnerability. At a deep level, it is a letting go of and a complete conversion from the addiction to, and idolatry of, power and control.

When the person who was wronged can share his or her pain with us, and realize that we truly know what they went through, they begin to feel understood. They begin to let go of the anger and resentment, the desire for revenge and the desire to punish. In short, the wronged party is starting to forgive us, because we have allowed that individual to empty themselves of their hurtful feelings and to make space for the spirit of forgiveness to flow through them and ultimately to us – then and only then can we legitimately ask for forgiveness. This is much more than just being sorry for the transgressions that one can excuse or mask as having been accidental. No, a genuine apology is an honest admission of responsibility for what happened. It invites us to look at why we did what we did. It might mean that we discover another defect of character that has been hidden or denied, and that awareness can take us back to Step One.

A genuine apology demands a commitment to change our behaviours and our belief system if necessary, so that we never repeat that same hurtful action again. An apology, in fact, is complete only when we can make a declaration to the other person that we will honestly try never to repeat that hurtful action. Marc Pizandawatc, mentioned in Part One, demonstrated how this declaration works during a training session of Returning to Spirit in Morley, Alberta.

Two trainees were late for a session one day, creating much tension in the room, since he never started a session until everyone was present, and he always started on time. When they finally appeared, blushing and apologizing profusely, Mark called upon different trainees to handle the situation. When no one addressed what he wanted, he took over and simply asked the two latecomers for their word that they would never be late again. They made that promise, and the session went on as if nothing happened.

Pizandawatc used this incident to teach the importance of a declaration. An apology is almost useless, he insisted, without a declaration, a promise to try to never repeat the hurtful behaviour. He underlined the difference between saying "I apologize for my hurtful actions" and saying "I apologize for my hurtful actions and give you my word that I will try never to do that again." Once the two latecomers had made their declaration, their apology was now complete.

Armed with this practical piece of wisdom, I decided to address a situation with a young couple with whom I had a strained relationship due to a misunderstanding. I had twice apologized to them previously, to no avail. The coolness and tension, especially on the part of the husband, was still very evident whenever we met.

Summoning up my courage, I called the husband, addressed the tension between us, renewed my apology, and this time, I added a declaration that I would honestly try to never again do what I had done. He became friendlier immediately, assured me that he would treat me more warmly now that he had my word, and we started talking about skiing. The rift that had festered for years was healed by means of that simple declaration.

I was amazed at what I had just experienced: the power of a declaration to complete an apology. I was also filled with joy and hope that this skill could help me grow in other areas of my life. Since then,

I have found this declaration to be a very effective way of seeking forgiveness and reconciliation from others (Steps Eight and Nine).

Forgiveness, Pardon and Reconciliation

There is an important distinction among these three that must be discussed here.

Forgiveness is letting go of anger and the desire for revenge. This we must do if we are to live free from destructive anger and in some degree of peace with ourselves and with others.

Pardon is letting go of a possible legal process. This is a choice. We do not have to pardon an abuser. We can forgive someone, and still prosecute or sue that person if that is what it will take to protect others, if there is danger that the person will reoffend, if there is a need for compensation or if this is what we need to do to bring closure to an incident.

Reconciliation is the ultimate goal. It is the restoration of a relationship when an apology is done well and forgiveness is extended. In fact, the relationship can grow stronger than the original relationship because of what the parties have been through and the amount of love manifested as humble honesty, apology and genuine forgiveness offered and accepted.

A simple way to apologize is to reverse the Step Six formula for forgiving someone. We can ask permission to share something with the offended person, and then remind them of our hurtful actions towards them. We then ask them how they felt and still feel about the incident, how it impacted them, and listen in such a way as to soak up their pain, however long that might take. Then we extend the apology, make a declaration to never repeat the hurtful behaviour and offer to make amends.

The biblical model for this is Matthew 5:23-24, quoted above, which states that if we are at the altar and recall that someone has a grudge against us, then we are to leave our gift at the altar, leave our worship and prayer, go to that person and make amends. For our Higher Power who is a loving God, relationship and reconciliation trump prayer and worship whenever there is a rift or hurtful event.

Those who cannot enter into this process of asking for forgiveness run the risk of addiction. Lacking faith, trust and courage, they most likely will continue to escape into an activity that will medicate their pain. That activity might be a very good thing, like culture and religion, but if it is used to avoid pain instead of dealing with pain, then chances are it will simply become another addiction.

Steps Eight and Nine work in tandem: Step Eight challenges us to get ready to make amends; Step Nine nudges us into making those amends through a genuine apology. This sincere apology is an open door to freedom from guilt, fear and loneliness. We have now worked through the core of the Twelve Step program, and are on the road to genuine freedom and serenity that no one can take away from us.

To conclude this section on Steps Four to Nine, I want to share an incident that will illustrate the power of these Steps as I applied them to a character defect of impatience that I came to know and to own.

I had always thought of myself as a patient person. However, one summer in Beauval, youth volunteers from St. Albert, Alberta, came to spend a month ministering to our youth. Two of the girls got hurt play-wrestling, and needed to be taken to the hospital over 100 kilometres away on rough gravel roads.

I was filled with resentment, although smiling all the time, and my speeding put them on edge. So did my passing a truck recklessly amid flying dust and stones. Two weeks later, at a prayer meeting in another community, one of the sisters told me that the driver of the truck that I had passed was the new administrator of the hospital. She was proceeding with caution due to lack of familiarity with the gravel road and the fragile nature of the goods she was transporting. Upon her arrival, she was telling the other sisters about a maniac in a green car who had passed her on the way up. Looking out the window just then, she saw me getting into the car and exclaimed, "That's him!"

I knew I was caught. I felt embarrassed and ashamed. For the next month, I tried to rationalize and justify my actions without success. I knew that our paths were going to cross, that this was unfinished business, and I needed to deal with it. Steps Eight and Nine helped me to make amends. In doing those steps, I was able to write the administrator a letter in which I admitted my impatience, apologized to her and made a commitment to her and to myself to heal from this defect of character, impatience, which took me back to Step One.

Some months later, when we met, we were able to laugh about this episode, though for a long time it was not a laughing matter to me. That incident and my process of writing a Step Nine letter helped me to grow and to deal with my impatience.

The core of Step Nine is the art of making a simple apology that carries a wealth of meaning and spirituality. Ultimately, an apology is a pure form of love: love for our neighbour whom we have hurt; love for ourselves by open, honest admission of guilt; and love for God who reciprocates with an even greater love. That circle of love is an experience of healing.

A sincere Step Nine leaves us with two key questions. First, to whom do I still need to make amends? Second, what do I need to heal in my life to avoid repeating that hurtful action? Step Nine is ultimately a commitment to continued growth and healing personally and relationally.

C. Living with the Program (Steps Ten to Twelve)

STEP TEN: Awareness

*Continued to take personal inventory
and when we were wrong promptly admitted it.*

Wash me thoroughly from my iniquity,
and cleanse me from my sin,
for I know my transgressions,
and my sin is ever before me. (Psalm 51:2-3)

*

The Twelve Step program encourages us to make Step Ten a daily reality in our life.

Have you ever driven a vehicle without a rear-view mirror? That mirror serves to help us drive forward more safely and securely. A speaker at a Roundup put it succinctly: "We need to look at the past, but we don't have to stare at it."

This is what a rear-view mirror does. It helps us glance backwards once in a while to make sure that all is okay behind us and that there is nothing there, such as a flashing red light that might negatively affect our forward progress.

Step Ten performs that function. We are invited to keep an eye on the past 24 hours, to monitor how we are doing. What did I say today? How did I act? Is there anyone whom I might have hurt in any way to whom I might owe an apology? Do I need to move towards forgiving someone who may have hurt me?

A good way to do Step Ten is to journal about the day. Reflect back on what transpired, with whom you interacted, the conversations you had, the activities you did. Was there any "stinking thinking"? Then check your emotions. Are there any feelings of guilt, shame or embarrassment? If there are, you may need to contact someone to see if there is a need to apologize and make amends. If this is impossible to do at the time, then you need to do it at the earliest possible moment.

Sometimes, this awareness may come our way in the form of feedback from a person we may have put off, hurt or offended in some way. Blessed are they who can humbly receive and accept this feedback, painful as it may be, as this is an opportunity for further growth and healing. It is sad when someone who is otherwise very intelligent, talented and accomplished resists and does not accept painful feedback from others. Such a person hinders his or her own growth through denial undergirded with false pride.

The Jesuits who specialize in retreat ministry and spiritual direction have developed a method of prayerfully looking back over one's day. The *Examination of Consciousness,* based on the writings of their founder, St. Ignatius of Loyola, involves the following steps: first, prayer for God's help to be with you; second, gratitude to God for the blessings of the day, savouring them; third, a review of the day, seeking awareness of how you did or did not accept God's grace in the events of that day; fourth, asking for forgiveness for any sins and wrongdoing; and fifth, prayer for the grace to follow God more closely the following day. Ignatius would suggest closing with the Our Father. The examen is a simple prayer of awareness as a way of noticing God's presence in the everyday events of life, and is a succinct summary of Ignatian spirituality.[45]

To return to the automobile maintenance metaphor, working Step Ten is like checking our oil. We have just finished living 24 hours as very complex human beings interacting with many other unique, very complex and sensitive human beings. Chances are that someone has been hurt by something we said or did. When operating a motor vehicle, one has to occasionally check fluid levels, batteries, belts, etc. to be sure the car keeps functioning well. Why would we not check our performance daily to see how we are functioning as human beings?

Step Ten asks us to promptly admit when we are wrong. Pizandawatc claims the newest addiction of the day is "Being Right." Authors of self-help and personal development books also mention this as an addiction. People would rather be right than happy.

Those with this addiction are convinced they are right and the other person is wrong. Often, so much energy goes into proving they are right that any possibility of a life-giving and rewarding relationship drops out of the picture. So do most of the pleasant feelings. This is unfortunate, because life is certainly more about having healthy relationships than about being right.

Step Ten provides us with a tremendous service in reminding us to "promptly admit it when we are wrong."

A quote from an anonymous source goes something like this: "When we are disturbed, no matter what the cause, there is something wrong with *us*." We need to go beyond rationalizations, to try to discover the true motives behind our actions and emotions, so that we can continue to learn, heal and grow on a daily basis. Step Ten can help us do just that.

STEP ELEVEN: Prayer

*Sought through prayer and meditation to improve
our conscious contact with God as we understood God,
praying only for the knowledge of God's will for us and the power
to carry that out.*

For this reason, since the day we heard it,
we have not ceased praying for you and asking that you may be
filled with the knowledge of God's will
in all spiritual wisdom and understanding,
so that you may lead lives worthy of the Lord,
fully pleasing to him, as you bear fruit in every good work
and as you grow in the knowledge of God.
(Colossians 1:9-10)

*

Step Eleven's power rests in its simplicity. When we pray, we need to ask God for two things only: what is God's will for us, and God's gift of strength to carry out that will.

Notwithstanding its simplicity, many people struggle with this step and the notion of prayer. Let us explore the reality of prayer to deepen our understanding and our experience of it.

We begin our exploration with a prayer by Thomas Merton, a Trappist monk:

> My Lord God, I have no idea where I am going. I do not see the road ahead of me. I cannot know for certain where it will end. Nor do I really know myself, and the fact that I think that I am following your will does not mean that I am actually doing so. But I believe that the desire to please you does in fact please you. And I hope I have that desire in all that I am doing. I hope that I will never do anything apart from that desire. And I know that if I do this you will lead me by the right road, though I may know nothing about it. Therefore I will trust you always though I may seem to be lost and in the shadow of death. I will not fear for you are ever with me, and you will never leave me to face my perils alone.[46]

In this humble prayer, we see that the desire to please God is, itself, effective prayer, and very much in line with Step Eleven – what is God's will for me?

Some interesting and thought-provoking definitions of prayer are the following:

Prayer is God-regarding, not self-regarding. *(Ruth Burroughs)*

Prayer is communication with God which involves mostly listening. *(Anonymous)*

Prayer is opening ourselves up to the unlimited possibilities of the presence of God continuing to create in us.[47]

Focusing on God as we understand God, listening to God's subtle communication through God's Word, nature, events, other people and silence are all elements of sincere, mature prayer. Keating writes, "Silence is the great common denominator between people, and also between us and God. God's first language is silence. Everything else is a poor translation. It is by entering into silence that we are best able to hear God."[48] Pondering what God is asking of us and communicating to us in that silence is profound prayer.

Conscious contact with God

A key element of Step Eleven is the phrase "sought to improve my conscious contact with God." *Illustration 18* is an image that can help us unwrap the implications of this comment. Life is like a pool of muskeg. Muskeg is the word used in the north to designate a bog or marshy land. In our woundedness, lack of trust and lack of faith, we struggle in spiritual muskeg to save ourselves by acting out of our emotions and practising our addictions. We keep this up until we are told that if we take one more drink, we will die, or lose our marriage, or something similar. We get sick and tired of being sick and tired. At that point, we can choose to stop struggling, and humbly cry out for help. God hears us, picks us up, lifts us out of the muskeg of our addiction and places us on an invisible slippery slope made up of twelve invisible spiritual steps.

Prayer: A Muskeg Image of Life

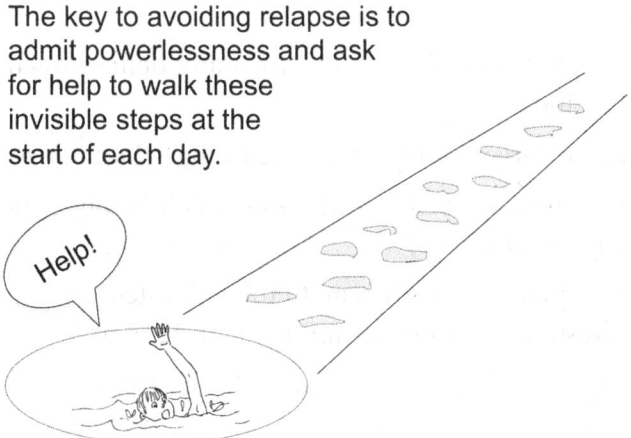

The key to avoiding relapse is to admit powerlessness and ask for help to walk these invisible steps at the start of each day.

Illustration 18

When some persons elect to start the trek through the Twelve Steps, often they do well enough through the first few steps. Then they become a little proud and begin to think that neither the steps nor the meetings nor a sponsor are necessary. Eventually, they stop working the program and lose their conscious contact with God. Not surprisingly, they relapse, fall off the wagon and end up back in the muskeg, struggling to save themselves once again.

This can go on and on and, for some, it becomes very repetitious. As mentioned earlier, I encountered one individual who had attended 14 rehabilitation centres. I am convinced that his was a *muskeg image* spirituality, repeatedly relying on his own power, relapsing and falling back into his addiction. The amazing progress he made once he understood the steps, and the Step Six and Step Nine letters he wrote, allowed him to leave behind any temptation to wallow in spiritual muskeg anymore.

Success lies in the ability to admit, at the beginning of each day, that we are powerless and need God's help just for that day. We must turn to our Higher Power for help and to establish conscious contact with God so that we will not slip or relapse. It is as simple as that.

If we respond, "Not today, maybe tomorrow," when someone asks us to drink or smoke up, the tomorrow never comes, and we won't slip.

Knowledge of God's will for us

One of the lines in the complete Serenity Prayer is "trusting that You will make all things right if I surrender to Your will." In the section about the Awareness Wheel, we saw the difference between being *willful* and *willing*. Our tendency in the past was to be willful, stubborn, insisting on our own will. Now we are invited to grow in our ability to be willing to cooperate with God's grace or Spirit, to let go of our own stubborn self-will and to submit to God's will for us.

In Step Three, we chose to surrender our wills and lives to the care of God as we understand God. Now we deepen that decision by praying that we might truly know what God's will is for us. No matter how earnestly we pray, God's will may not be clear. It often takes discernment to sort out what God's will is among all the possible options open to us.

Masters of the spiritual life write and speak about the experience of consolation and desolation when it comes to discernment. However, both experiences need some explanation. Not all pleasant feelings are consolation, and not all unpleasant feelings are desolation. Discernment helps us to determine which is which, and what extent or magnitude to apportion to it.

Usually, consolation is the serenity and peace that accompanies a choice to do God's will with the comforting belief that God is pleased with our choice. It is a gift from the Spirit of God, a profound reality not dependent on the surrounding environment. This is not the same as a fleeting feeling of happiness and excitement.

Desolation can also be a learning moment in that God gives us an experience of the *apparent absence* of God to assist us in avoiding certain decisions or actions and to understand more deeply what it means to grow in faith. This is not the same as depression.

Desolation may take the form of a deep, dark spiritual experience. As Gerald May wrote, basing his observation on St. John of the

Cross, "a true spiritual dark night is characterized by deep humility and by continuing service to others in spite of one's own interior pain and confusion."[49]

The bottom line is that we need to pray for the knowledge of what God's will is for us, and for the power or spiritual strength to carry that out.

Power to carry it out

Knowing what God's will is for us is only one part. Next, we have to muster up the courage and strength to do God's will, even if doing so will stretch us or if it is something that we don't really want to do.

Recall when Jesus prayed in the Garden of Gethsemane, "Father, let this cup pass me by. Nevertheless, not my will but your will be done" (Matthew 26:39). He was rooted in prayer, in an intimate relationship with the Father. He knew that he had come from the Father and that he was returning to the Father. What a powerful example of knowing God's will and carrying it out, knowing the result was pain and death. Jesus was utterly convinced of God's love for him, even if he later experienced only the dark night, the desolation, the apparent absence of God on the cross, as he cried out, "My God, my God, why have you forsaken me?" (Matthew 27:46).

That cry from the cross is not evidence of a lack of faith, but rather is an example of the power of faith to carry out the will of God. Jesus was asked, not so much to die on the cross, but to demonstrate the depth of God's love for us through the total gift of his life for us given up on the cross. His knowledge of God's will for him and his rootedness in how loved he was by God gave him the power to carry out that sacrifice. On the cross, Jesus was able to forgive those who had rejected and persecuted him and were now crucifying him, as he uttered the words "Father, forgive them, for they know not what they do."

Someone who experienced this dark night was Mother Teresa of Calcutta. Although her struggle was not visible on the outside, she experienced only the apparent absence of God for over 50 years, as she carried on joyfully ministering to the poor and dying of India. Her faith was so strong that she was given the supreme test of faith that Jesus experienced on the cross. This is the test that we who are weaker in faith ask to avoid when we pray in the Our Father, "Lead us not into temptation."

The bottom line of Step Eleven is that we are rooted, through prayer and meditation, in an experience of our Higher Power's love for us. This in turn sheds light on God's will for us, and gives us the power to carry out that will, whatever the cost to us, as it did for Jesus on the cross. That power is rooted in prayer.

Ways of praying

Spiritual writers distinguish three ways or modes of prayer: saying prayers, meditation and contemplation.

The first two modes are discursive, a word that comes from a Latin verb meaning to run about or to go from one thing to another. In discursive prayer, we are the subjects and the agents of the act of prayer. We *say* prayers: the Serenity Prayer, the Our Father, etc. There is usually some analytical reasoning involved, something that we *do*. The noun "discourse" implies conversation, the verbal interchange of ideas presented in an orderly and somewhat extended fashion. We *meditate* on these ideas, and consider our spiritual needs or virtues. In other words, in discursive prayer, we *pray*.

In contemplation, the third modality of prayer, God is both the subject and the agent of our prayer. We remain receptive to God's activity within us. God prays in us. We are *prayed*. There are some beautiful scripture passages that capture the essence of this kind of prayer, such as "The Lord will fight for you; you have only to keep still" (Exodus 14:14).

Beginners in prayer tend to use a more discursive style of prayer. That is to be expected. The danger, however, is to remain there and to think this is all there is to it, to limit ourselves to that kind of prayer only. Some of us are ready for a different, more mature kind of prayer.

One day a woman called and complained that she could no longer pray. Nothing seemed to appeal to her. I knew how profound her Twelve Step healing journey had been, and I suspected that her problem was not an inability to pray, but rather that she was ready for a more mature kind of prayer. I introduced her to *Lectio Divina*, and she was set free to grow in her relationship with the Higher Power in a way that met her needs.

Lectio Divina

The term itself means "holy reading." *Lectio Divina* has a long history and is associated with the followers of St. Benedict. In the sixth century, Benedict inherited a method of praying from the monk John Cassian. John lived with the Desert Fathers in Egypt. His aim was unceasing prayer through the repetition of a word or phrase chosen from scripture. This word or phrase was repeated over and over, until it became rooted in the heart. These early monks thought that idleness was an enemy, and they used manual labour and prayerful reading as ways of growing spiritually. They simply did it and took it for granted, without really seeing it as a method.

In the 12th century, the Carthusian Guigo II, abbot of Grande Chartreuse, taught in his celebrated booklet *Jacob's Ladder* an ordered method of *Lectio Divina*.[50] He presented it as a ladder for climbing to heaven. Abbot Guigo pointed out four rungs: reading, meditation, prayer and contemplation, though in no particular order. He used the image of food to explain it: reading is the food, meditation is chewing the food, prayer is enjoying the flavour, and contemplation embraces and nourishes the hungry soul.

This method of praying is analogous to developing a personal relationship. We can only love what we know. A relationship involves being with the other, talking, listening, sharing from the heart and wasting time together. It is a process that takes time. So does contemplative prayer. Spiritual teachers see it as the most integrated way of praying, blending Eastern and Western spirituality. Former Abbot Thomas Keating underlines its healing power even at the level of the unconscious. We now explore at a greater depth how it is done.

1. Lectio (Holy Reading)

Read a scripture passage or a portion of program literature prayerfully, not to gather information or to finish, but until the heart is touched. Choose a word or phrase that strikes you as a mantra to pray with.

2. Meditatio (Meditation)

Begin this stage when your heart is touched. Stop reading, think about the passage and mull over the passage a bit. Welcome what has touched you and wrestle with it. Ask what God is saying to you through the passage. Allow the passage to nourish you, to connect with your life. Use your imagination and intellect. Get into the scene, explore your feelings, play around with the passage, personalize it and visualize it. Consult the footnotes or a commentary on the passage. Share your thoughts, questions and feelings with others, if you are praying in a group.

3. Oratio (Prayer)

Pray with the passage. Respond personally when your heart is touched. Dialogue with God and speak to God. Be intimate with God. Lift up your mind and heart to God. Feel your emotions, perhaps even awe and rejoicing. Weep, shed tears, express petitions, sing and express the emotions. Kneel, stand or lie down – any posture you desire. Above all, pray for others and for your own needs, using the words of the passage.

4. Contemplatio (Contemplation)

This final stage is just "being with" God. Use the word or phrase that struck you earlier in the *lectio* part as a mantra. Be mindful and still. Be aware of your breathing. Start saying the mantra as you breathe in. Try not to think or feel anything. The goal of this prayer is to simply be in God's presence and believe that God is doing whatever God wants to do within you. This takes faith.

When a thought or a feeling comes to the surface, do not cling to it. Resist the temptation to own it, to record it. Simply acknowledge the thought, idea or feeling. Thank God for it, then place it gently into an imaginary canoe, let it drift away and return to your mantra.

If it was a genuine inspiration from the Lord, it will come back to you later. Eventually, try to even let go of the mantra, and "just be" in God's presence.

For someone who is a workaholic, this is a helpful way to pray, as in this prayer, one does nothing except pray the mantra or just be, like a sunflower following the sun. One does not try to achieve anything in this prayer, other than to simply rest in God's presence and "Be still and know that God is God" (Psalm 46:10).

This level of prayer, contemplation, is somewhat rare in our world today. It is also so counter-cultural and difficult to comprehend for the modern person that it merits more discussion. Here is a reflection on contemplation by Gerald May:

> Silence is the one "technique" or discipline that is constant through all contemplative traditions. It seems to be the fundamental activity that people can perform in themselves in the service of their own spiritual awakening.
>
> ... There are elements of practicing a 'right relationship' in meditation and contemplative prayer. The practice of quiet is an exercise in 'not-doing' ... a study in surrender and willingness, a discipline of letting go. Each time we sit quietly, the silence takes us as far as we can go at that moment toward the loosening of our preconceived images of ourselves, and it teaches us as much as we can learn about the fallibilities of dualistic thought.
>
> ... One cannot expect to grow in spiritual awareness without some intentional practice of silence.... Contemplative prayer is best viewed as nothing other than preparing oneself in willingness for appreciation of closeness to God, whether or not this appreciation is actually experienced.[51]

A more visual way of looking at the importance of prayer is to compare it to the need to constantly check the gas gauge in a vehicle while on a journey. This is almost a reflex action for most. Those who do not do this face the risk of running out of gas before they reach their destination or when they need it. Prayer, then, is like gassing up spiritually.

Again, the art of living 24 hours is much more risky and complicated than driving a car. What more practical way is there to assure that we don't run out of the spiritual energy and love needed to deal with the challenges of life than by praying each day, especially in the mornings, to charge up our spiritual batteries, like solar batteries that need the power of the sun to shine at night?

Prayer of the Anawim

The Hebrew word *anawim* refers to the poor of every sort: the vulnerable, the marginalized, the socio-economically oppressed, those of lowly status without earthly power. These are the simple folks among whom Jesus was born and raised: people like Joseph and Mary, Zechariah and Elizabeth, his grandparents, Joachim and Anne, and the Apostles. According to Sr. Joan L. Roccasalvo, C.S.J.,

> the anawim depended totally on God for whatever they owned. The word *anawim* (*inwetan*) means those who are bowed down. Mahatma Gandhi understood *inwetan* as the way of *bhakti*, that is, loving devotion and surrender to God. In times of suffering, the *anawim* remained faithful and awaited the good things of the Lord to fill their emptiness, as the Lucan gospel tells us in (Lk 1:53). They delighted in the Lord because they were rooted in him.[52]

One of my favourite biblical episodes about this kind of prayer is that of Peter walking on the water (Matthew 14:28-32). Peter has a certain degree of faith when he sees Jesus coming towards the disciples on the water, and he says, "Lord, make me come to you on the water."

This is prayer, but in a way it is a proud prayer. Peter is telling Jesus what he wants Jesus to do for him, and this is all too typical of most of our attempts to pray. However, Jesus humours him and tells him to come. To his credit, Peter has enough faith to step out of the boat and start walking on the water.

I think I know what happened next, because I am so much like Peter. He probably got proud of what he was doing, looked back at the boat to see if his friends were watching, started showing off a bit, took his eyes off Jesus (the source of his power), felt the wind and suddenly started to sink. He was drowning. He knew that no one else but Jesus could save him, so he blurted out just three words: "Lord, save me!" This time, his prayer was humble. This prayer came from his poverty, his powerlessness and his need. And suddenly, Jesus was there, taking him by the shoulder, lifting him up and saying only, "O you of little faith, why did you doubt?"

How do you think Peter responded to that statement? I doubt that Peter told Jesus that he could do it on his own again, and let go of him. To the contrary, I am convinced that Peter hung on to Jesus, and together they walked back to the boat.

"Walking with Jesus" is the key to prayer for the addicted person, and is the meaning of "conscious contact with God." Using our own power, there is no way we can live each day the way God wants us to. We must admit our need and grab onto our Higher Power, each day, each morning, one day at a time, before we get into trouble.

Praying this way over the years within the context of the Twelve Step program has led me to outline a method for prayer in response to a request by someone who wanted to grow in her prayer life. This method is something that I call Twelve by Twenty-Four. It is presented in Appendix 4.

This simple prayer format has been instrumental in helping me work all Twelve Steps daily. I share it with you as an invitation for you to use it for yourself or to develop something similar that might be better suited to you.

These thoughts on Step Eleven do not really do justice to such a profound Step. I hope, however, they will help the reader to come to a deeper appreciation of both the depth of this Step, as well as the need to live it out in daily life.

STEP TWELVE: Sharing and Service

Having had a spiritual awakening as the result of these steps, we tried to carry this message to alcoholics (others), and to practice these principles in all our affairs.

You know how an alien feels, for you were once aliens in Egypt.
(Exodus 23:9)
"Once you have recovered, you must now help your brothers."
(Luke 22:31-34)

*

If you're green, you grow; if you're not, you rot!

Make Step Twelve an integral part of your life, and you will keep on growing.

"Love is only love when you give it away." This saying applies especially to the Twelve Step program: happy, free sobriety is really only yours when you share it with others. Step Twelve invites us to solidify our new-found freedom by sharing it with others and by following some basic principles that truly become our way of life.

Having had a spiritual awakening

The late spiritual writer Anthony de Mello stressed the importance of being awake, of waking up. All too many people go through life barely aware of the reality and beauty of God's creation all around them, and too preoccupied with their problems and difficulties to see anything else.

I remember feeling slighted one day when an elder walking by ignored my greeting. Years later, with more experience of life behind me, I realized that, as an active alcoholic, he was so burdened and so focused on surviving for one more day in his blurred state that he did not hear me, or if he did, my words were only background noise that was meaningless and incomprehensible to him.

The recovering addict, on the other hand, has experienced the liberating power of God that our Higher Power wants for all people. By working the steps diligently, addicts find that God has done for them what they could never have done on their own: sustain a life of sobriety, joyous and free.

We tried to carry this message to alcoholics (others)

God needs us to witness to this liberating power and to invite others to share in it. Sharing this experience is not only the right thing to do, it keeps it fresh for us and keeps us learning, healing and growing.

That was the experience of Bill W., as he put it: "In the first six months of my own sobriety, I worked hard with many alcoholics. Not a one responded. Yet this work kept me sober. It wasn't a question of those alcoholics giving me anything. My stability came out of trying to give, not out of demanding that I receive."[53]

The early days of Alcoholics Anonymous, when men and women spared no effort to meet sometimes nightly, to support one another and to reach out to others, are very inspirational and educational. Having had a spiritual experience, they *tried* to spread the message to others by sharing their experience. The Big Book motivates those who are fearful by encouraging them to "cling to the thought that, in God's hands, the dark past is the greatest possession you have – the key to life and happiness for others. With it you can avert death and misery for them."[54] That statement captures the challenge of Step Twelve. God does not ask us to succeed, only to believe and to reach out, and God will do the rest.

Practise these principles in all our affairs

The Twelve Step program can and should become a new way of life for us. As we reflect on this step, what might be good to keep in mind are the words found on the sobriety medallions: *To Thy Own Self Be True* and *Recovery, Unity, Service*. These are perhaps the most basic principles that we need to practise to maintain a life of happy, free sobriety.

These words define what the Twelve Steps entail. The first phrase reminds us of the need for rigorous honesty and the challenge to discover our True Selves. Then we focus on stopping the addictive behaviour, or *recovery*. This goal is fundamental.

We never recover alone, however, but only within the warmth of fellowship or *unity*. Sponsors play a key role, as do the meetings, where we share feelings about the steps that we are working on and the experiences encountered.

The underlying foundation for these two elements of recovery and unity is *service*, giving away what we have found as the best way of keeping it. Winston Churchill, I believe, coined the phrase "We make a living by what we get; we make a life by what we give away." Step Twelve applies the basic principle that by trying to help others, whether we are successful or not, we help ourselves. It is in losing ourselves and sharing the gift of our sobriety that we end up keeping it.

The Big Book describes the experience of living Step Twelve this way:

> You will make lifelong friends. You will be bound to them with new and wonderful ties, for you will escape disaster together and you will commence shoulder to shoulder your common journey. Then you will know what it means to give yourself that others may survive and rediscover life. You will learn the full meaning of "Love thy neighbor as thyself."[55]

Step Twelve is expressed biblically by the Old Testament passage about the crossing of the Jordan into the Promised Land: "I will put at your mercy the Canaanites, the Amorites, the Hittites, the Perizzites, the Hivites, the Girgashites and the Jebusites" (Joshua 24:11-12). The people were warned by this passage that they were not finished yet, even though they had arrived in the Promised Land. They would still have to contend with seven enemies. For me, the character defects and painful emotions that require continued attention and healing are the enemies that still exist once one has completed the steps for a first time, and even after many times. These enemies could be linked to the seven deadly sins that are part of the traditional teaching of the Church: pride, greed, lust, anger, gluttony, envy and sloth.

One of the best weapons we have for waging a spiritual battle against these subtle, cunning, baffling and powerful enemies is the Twelve Step program, worked diligently. To use a sporting phrase, the best defence is a strong offence. The program is a great offence.

The Twelve Step program was designed to assist alcoholics in subduing an addiction and embarking upon an addictions-free lifestyle. The principles underlying these steps apply to all life matters, and deserve consideration in all of our human endeavours.

I like to compare the Twelve Step program to a 12-string guitar. All the strings can be strummed at once, or only one or a few are fingered at any one time. They all make for beautiful music, however they are played, as long as they are all played. The Twelve Step program is meant to create a beautiful melody out of our once battered and bruised lives.

Suggested Activities

1. Which step seems to stand out for you, perhaps to the point of being uncomfortable? Journal with that particular step. Keep writing for a good 20 minutes without stopping. Write down everything that comes to your mind: write down your feelings, etc. If you stop before the end of the 20 minutes, read the content of that particular step again, and then continue to write whatever surfaces, even if it is a repeat of what you have already written.

2. Now take your journalling to prayer. As you pray with it, what seems to repeat itself, stand out and truly take hold of you? Spend time with where this "awareness" tends to lead you. What do you see yourself needing to do with this knowledge?

3. Choose a scripture passage or a passage from some program literature, and take some time to practise the *Lectio Divina* method of prayer. Share with someone else the result of that prayer time.

PART FIVE: Understanding and Integrating The Twelve Steps

The Recovery Wheel

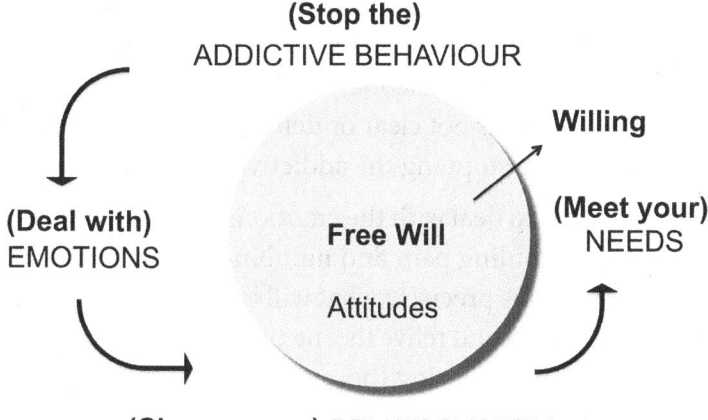

Illustration 19

In Part One, we looked at the Awareness Wheel that taught us how human beings function in terms of vision, belief systems, emotions and behaviour. That image then became the Wellness Wheel, comprised of met needs, positive belief systems, pleasant emotions and constructive behaviour. In Part Three, the wheel became the Dysfunctional Wheel of unmet needs, warped belief systems, painful emotions and destructive behaviour.

Coming full circle, the wheel now becomes the Recovery Wheel. To heal and become healthy, we reverse the direction of the Dysfunctional Wheel by stopping the addictive behaviour, dealing with our emotions, changing our belief system and, finally, finding ways to fulfill our human love needs.

First, we must stop the addictive behaviour. It is nearly impossible to embark on a healing journey without hitting bottom and letting go of the actions that are hurting us and others. If we are dealing with a chemical addiction, we stop drinking or taking the drug. If we are dealing with a process addiction, such as gambling, we stop that activity.

In situations involving both chemical and process addiction in the same person at the same time, the imperative to stop the addictive behaviour can seem questionable. Should one stop drinking or drugging before dealing with codependency, or would treatment for codependency first help someone who can't say "no" to peers stop drinking? The answer is not clear or definitive, though most professionals would advise stopping the addictive behaviour first.

The next step is to deal with the emotions. Since addictive behaviour is all about avoiding pain and numbing our painful emotions, turning this around is precisely what will begin the healing process. We need to remember and relive the memories, feel the emotions and stay with the feelings. Sharing those painful emotions with trusted others helps diffuse their control over us.

From there, one moves on to address our warped belief systems or our "stinking thinking," as the Big Book puts it. Here, counselling, lectures, cognitive therapy and correct information on addiction will play a part.

Changing our belief system does not mean changing one's religion, if one is part of a faith community, but rather means adopting more positive attitudes. It can also mean changing our "Way of Being" and how we perceive the world.

I recall an incident during which I became painfully aware of my need to change my belief system. Our ministry team was offering a

Christopher Leadership Course on effective speaking in one of the communities that we served. One night during the course, I noticed that one of the team members was no longer talking to me. Her silent treatment continued throughout the next evening. Finally, I could no longer stand the silence, so I asked her if there was something wrong. She asked if I really wanted to know. I replied that I very much did want to know. She shared with me how hurt she felt by my conduct, by the way that I was controlling everything, changing the plans of the other instructors, and even changing the chairs that they had set up.

I soaked up her pain as she shared her emotions with me. I apologized, and asked quietly what I could do to improve things. She replied quickly and firmly, "Change your belief system." I was startled, and asked what she meant. She asked me if I really believed that my way was the best way. Did I not see that perhaps someone else's way might be just as effective? Did it have to always be my way?

I sheepishly had to admit that she was right, and that I had some work to do to change the way I behave when I'm under stress and my perfectionism takes over. I realized that my need to have my way was kicking in and taking its toll. It would not be easy, I knew, but at least I was willing to try, and I made that commitment to her.

I also shared with her how hurt and angry I felt that she chose to give me the silent treatment for so long rather than sharing her feelings with me right away. She apologized for not expressing her frustration to me earlier and for letting it build up into days of silent treatment. We were reconciled through this honest exchange, and the rest of the course went well.

Integrating the Twelve Steps

With that brief comment on the Recovery Wheel in the background, we can now turn our attention to integrating the Twelve Steps into a healthy lifestyle. As I progressed through the steps as a young adult, I seemed to stumble after my Step Five. I had very little understanding or comprehension of how to proceed with Step Six. I was also aware that I was not alone. Many rehabilitation centres that use the steps release their clients after they complete their Step

Five. There is precious little help for those who want to move on with the rest of the steps, and so many people stop growing at that point. They start only to maintain sobriety, which is not really recovery. They need to move on to find a way to work all the steps, especially Steps Six to Twelve.

This section will seek to deepen our understanding of the Twelve Steps, how they build on each other and how they interrelate as we strum each of the 12 strings of our sobriety guitar on our way to a new and lasting way of life.

The Twelve Steps Applied to Teepee Spirituality

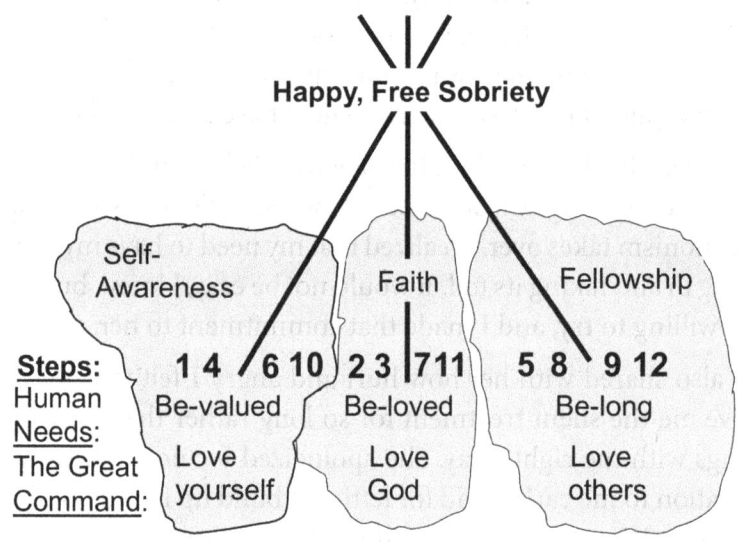

Illustration 20

It's easy to talk about recovery and spirituality, but the recovering person must always face the difficult reality and ask how they can integrate what they are learning once the lecture is over. The concept of Teepee Spirituality, presented in Part Two, points out the need to walk in harmony and to balance the three poles of Faith, Self-awareness and Fellowship. How can the recovering person effectively achieve this goal? The answer is simple. Work the Twelve Steps.

Making connections between the familiar and the new is one of the joys of the learning process for adults. After months of thinking about Teepee Spirituality and sharing it with others, I suddenly discovered the connection between this concept and the Twelve Steps. If we use the steps as imaginary pegs to secure the teepee, they fit perfectly.

As shown in this illustration, simply by working the steps, the recovering person will find the balance between faith, fellowship and self-awareness, and will integrate this concept of Teepee Spirituality into his or her own life.

Around the centre pole of *Faith* are the steps that involve our relationship with God as we understand God: Step Two (belief in a Higher Power), Step Three (surrender to God), Step Seven (humble prayer for healing) and Step Eleven (daily prayer and meditation). Anytime we work these steps, we grow in our relationship with God, learning to love God and letting ourselves be loved by God.

Around the pole of *Fellowship* are the steps that involve our relationship with others: Step Five (admitting our wrongdoing to another human being), Step Eight (listing those we had harmed by our actions), Step Nine (making amends to those we had hurt) and Step Twelve (sharing our spiritual experience and message of sobriety with others). Every time we work these steps, we grow in our relationship with others and allow ourselves to be loved. We will meet our deep human need to belong to others, and will fulfill the great command to love others.

What deeper fellowship could there be than Step Five, admitting to another human being, in trust and honesty, the exact nature of our wrongs? Those who assist program members with a Step Five can attest to how moving, profound and life-giving this experience can be.

Equally profound is the fellowship involved in Steps Eight and Nine: going to another human being, totally vulnerable, admitting past actions that have hurt that person, listening to them share how they were hurt, then humbly asking for forgiveness and seeking to make amends to the extent possible.

Step Twelve ensures a lifetime of constant growth in fellowship with others, as one daily shares one's spiritual experience with all who will listen. Truly, working these four steps involving fellowship is a simple and sure path towards healing relationships.

Around the pole of *Self-awareness* are the steps that involve our relationships with ourselves: Step One (admitted powerlessness), Step Four (searching and fearless moral inventory), Step Six (awareness of defects of character) and Step Ten (daily moral inventory). Every time we work these steps, we grow in our relationship with ourselves, learning self-love and self-acceptance.

Now we can make a connection and learn. What is striking about this illustration? Perhaps you have already noticed that there are four steps under each pole of the teepee. Four of the steps have to do with faith and prayer. Four of the steps have to do with fellowship, and four of the steps have to do with self-awareness. This balance and harmony about the Twelve Steps is remarkable.

Regarding connections, a First Nations resident helped me learn more about this concept during a lecture one day. I had clustered the steps around their appropriate poles. He suggested that I string them out along the bottom and connect each with the top, making a pole out of each one of them, and thus completing a teepee using 15 poles.

The connection that traditionally there are 15 poles used in a teepee and 15 poles in this arrangement of Teepee Spirituality came to us all at once. The room was filled with grateful excitement and joy as we all learned collaboratively a bit more about our own recovery in the light of First Nations spirituality.

In summary, working and following the Twelve Steps will lead us to fulfill the great commandment of love, and our deepest human needs will be met. We will blossom as happy, free, whole human beings, all by simply following the guidance of the Twelve Step program. It works, if you work it!

The Recovery Burger

Another image that can help us to understand how the program works is the Recovery Burger. The top bun is what we first see when

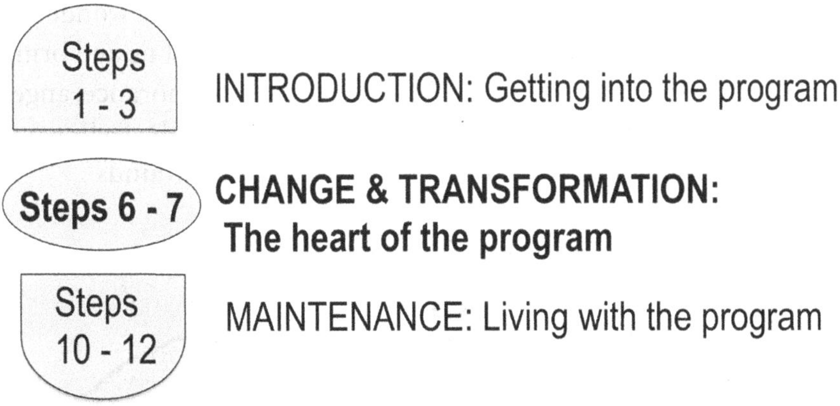

Part Five: Understanding and Integrating The Twelve Steps

Steps 1 - 3   INTRODUCTION: Getting into the program

Steps 6 - 7   **CHANGE & TRANSFORMATION:** **The heart of the program**

Steps 10 - 12   MAINTENANCE: Living with the program

Illustration 21

we open a hamburger. That bun represents Steps One to Three of the program. These steps are simply an introduction to the power of the program, yet many people never get past these three first steps. They are stuck in the introduction, which is like chewing on dry bread.

Years ago, I asked a local fisherman who was participating in a Twelve Step workshop how long he had been sober. He replied proudly, "Twenty-three years, Father." Congratulating him, I then asked him what step he was on. His answer was much more subdued: "Step One." I turned to his wife sitting next to him and jokingly but deliberately asked her if he was on a dry drunk. She vigorously nodded affirmatively. Apparently that got through to the man, as the next time I saw him he was quick to inform me that he was now on Step Three.

The bottom bun of the hamburger, Steps Ten to Twelve, is living with the program through a daily moral inventory, daily prayer and meditation, and sharing our experience of sobriety with others on a daily basis. The temptation is to jump from Step One to Step Twelve, organizing and chairing meetings, without really working the steps in between; this is a recipe for relapse.

The patty is the meat of the program, Steps Four to Nine, where healing, change and growth really begin to happen. How unfortunate that so many people are either afraid of these steps or do not understand how they really work, especially Steps Six and Seven.

The remainder of this book will try to shed light on the wonderful power of these steps, the meat of the program, to heal us and bring us new life. The choice is ours. We can stay stuck in ignorance, anger and grief, or move on to healthy grieving and recovery by feeling our emotions, dealing with our defects and healing our wounds.

Our Spiritual Burden and the Twelve Steps

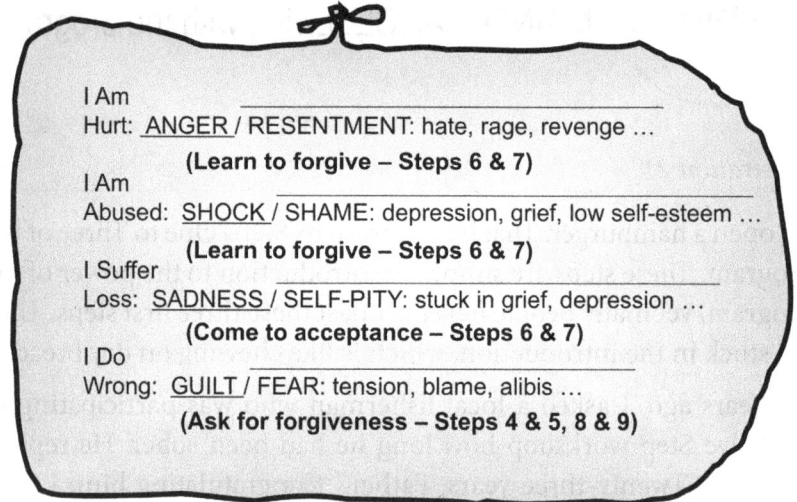

Illustration 22

We now return to the Spiritual Burden presented at the end of Part Three to see how the Twelve Steps can liberate us from the invisible burden that many people carry through life. As a reminder, anger, resentment, shock, shame, sadness, self-pity, guilt and fear fill the invisible but very real garbage bag that weighs down our thoughts, our actions and our spirits. It is this very specific burden that Steps Four to Nine, the core of the program, are designed to heal. Let us apply the steps to the schema presented in *Illustration 12* of Part Three:

Anger and resentment are two of our biggest and most common defects of character. The best way to let go of *anger* and *resentment* and all the related painful emotions that flow from being hurt is to learn to forgive. Learning to forgive those who hurt us, as a way to liberation from anger and resentment, is what Steps Six and Seven are all about.

The best way to let go of *shock* and *shame* and all the concomitant painful emotions that flow from the trauma of being sexually abused is to learn to forgive our abusers. Letting go of the desire for revenge as a way to regain our dignity and innocence is also what Steps Six and Seven are all about.

The best way to let go of crippling *sadness* and *self-pity*, and all the related painful emotions that accompany them, is to learn to mourn and grieve, and finally to accept our losses. Acceptance is a form of forgiveness, and this too is what Steps Six and Seven will help us to do.

Finally, the best way to let go of *guilt* and *fear* and all the related painful emotions that go with having done wrong by acting out of our painful emotions instead of forgiving is to simply admit the wrong that we have done. It is to learn to apologize; to soak up the pain of those we have hurt; to ask for forgiveness; to make a declaration to change; and, as best we can, make amends for the harm that was done. That is what Steps Four, Five, Eight and Nine will accomplish within us.

In the end, working Steps Four to Nine is one of the best ways to get rid of the spiritual burden and invisible garbage bag that we carry all too often through our daily lives. These steps are a practical way to learn to forgive, to accept and to ask for forgiveness. That is why they form the core of the program and why those who balk at them and try to find a softer, easier way never really rid themselves of their spiritual burden.

The Healing Hamburger

A Healing Hamburger image of the program is one of the best ways I have found to mentally picture the Twelve Steps, to see their relationship and to understand the inner dynamic of each step. It is simply an expansion of the Recovery Burger of *Illustration 21*.

Steps 1 - 3	INTRODUCTION: Getting into the program
Steps 4 - 5	REPENTANCE: experiencing forgiveness from God, myself and one other person
Steps 6 - 7	**HEALING: learning how to forgive those who have hurt me in any way**
Steps 8 - 9	RECONCILIATION: apologizing to and experiencing forgiveness from all those I have hurt
Steps 10 - 12	MAINTENANCE: living with the program on a daily basis

Illustration 23

The Healing Hamburger has the same top and bottom buns, but now there are three meat patties, each of which has distinct functions and flavours that lead to healing.

Steps Four and Five are the part of the hamburger in which we experience forgiveness from God, from those we harmed and from ourselves. One of the most challenging obstacles to personal freedom is our refusal to forgive ourselves for our actions. The naming of our wrongdoing in Step Four and hearing ourselves say it to another are the beginnings of the process of healing ourselves.

Steps Eight and Nine are where we experience more forgiveness, only now from others. These steps expand Steps Four and Five into a broad circle of love with others that leads to the possibility of reconciliation and deep, renewed fellowship with others.

Steps Six and Seven are where we experience healing as the power of forgiving others. We get in touch with how we have been hurt and how we reacted negatively in our inability to forgive. We start to let go of the anger, sadness and grief. We learn to forgive all those who hurt us and to accept all the losses of life that come our way. This truly is the core of the program.

A final note before moving on may be helpful. Even the way we eat a hamburger can give us an insight into how to work the program. Initially, when new to the program, we more or less work through the steps chronologically. However, the steps are alive and dynamic, fluid and flexible, interrelated, adaptable and connected to our lives, which are also dynamic and unpredictable. To restrain oneself to a linear approach to the steps would be too constricting, too removed from how life unfolds.

The most satisfying way to work the program is similar to how one eats a hamburger. We bite through the whole hamburger to get the whole flavour. No one eats the top bun first, then the meat, and finally the bottom bun.

It's the same with the steps. As one becomes more familiar with them, one can work almost all the steps every day, simultaneously. They begin to fit into the everyday nooks and crannies of one's life in a dynamic fashion. We go on digesting the whole program, one day at a time, one bite at a time – spiritual nourishment for the rest of our lives.

Like playing the 12-string guitar, working all Twelve Steps is the best way to make a beautiful melody out of the notes that life gives us. Anything less is to cheat ourselves out of the richness of the program and the fullness of the symphony of our lives that God intends for us. The "Twelve by Twenty-Four" format for daily prayer mentioned in Part Four and found in the appendix is one way of living this out.

A Spirituality of Weeding

Illustration 24 provides another perspective of how the steps work in our lives. This illustration takes us back to the healing that I experienced after the healing Eucharist recounted earlier (see p. 152). We are born into a wounded, dysfunctional world. While we are in our mother's womb, the lack of love in our less-than-perfect families begins to influence us negatively. This manifests itself in the most painful and basic emotion, human insecurity. Then we begin to feel anger and resentment towards the source of that hurt.

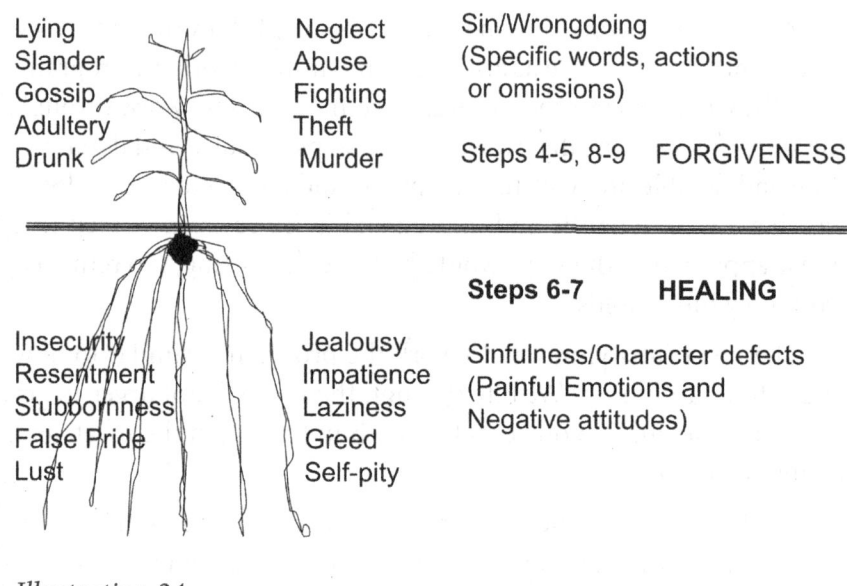

Illustration 24

Our unconditional loyalty to our parents and our inability to articulate our feelings lead us to deny that these painful emotions even exist. We start to feel jealous of others who seem to enjoy the love that we are not experiencing. We stubbornly cling to our own notions of right or wrong. We also begin to feel shame and embarrassment at what has happened to us, especially if there has been abuse. Other painful realities that creep into our lives might be impatience, bad temper, stubbornness, despair, greed and self-pity. The traditional seven deadly sins mentioned in Part Four would fit in here, as well as the comments of Jesus in Mark 7:21-23.

In short, we begin to develop deep roots of character defects as a way to survive. All this is within us, below the surface, as we become a ball of painful emotions and negative attitudes. Healing is needed: this is what Steps Six and Seven are all about.

As was just mentioned, being slavish to the chronology of the steps is not always necessary, but before we work Steps Six and Seven, it is advisable to address the surface weeds of our wrongdoing, those actions for which we can assume responsibility. We act out of our pain as a way to protect ourselves and survive. This involves hurting others and then suffering the subsequent emotions of guilt and fear. Our wrongdoing is all the specific negative actions, words, thoughts and omissions that we have committed out of our pain.

For all of our wrongdoing, there is forgiveness through Steps Four, Five, Eight and Nine. We admit our wrongdoing to ourselves, to God and finally to another human being. Then we make amends for what we did wrong. Now, plunging deeper within, we find that Steps Six and Seven offer profound healing of our negative attitudes and painful emotions.

The biblical model of working the Twelve Steps is the raising of Lazarus in Luke 11. Jesus first waits until Lazarus has died; then he strengthens Martha's faith in his power to act on behalf of her brother that very day (and not just at the end of time, as she states). That is what Steps One to Three do for us. Jesus waits until we are ready, and strengthens our faith. Then Jesus commands that the stone be removed. (He relies on the community to do that, rather than do it himself.) This is what Steps Four and Five accomplish within us. Now it is his turn. Jesus looks up, prays to the Father with confident gratitude and speaks words of new life to Lazarus: "Lazarus, come out." And Lazarus comes out, alive once again! This is what Steps Six and Seven will do for us. In a mysterious way, sometimes without our even being aware of it, God reaches deep within us and pulls out of us a deeply rooted defect of character by filling us with a related gift of the Holy Spirit.

Lazarus is raised back to life, but he stinks, is all bound up in burial cloth, is unable to see with his head covered and is barely able to walk. There is no point in being alive if we are bound up, as Lazarus was when he emerged from the tomb (like a dry drunk). So Jesus relies on the community again, and commands that he be unbound and set free. This is what Steps Eight to Twelve will do for us as we work them. They will unbind us and help us to enjoy happy, free sobriety.

Taken together, these Twelve Steps, and especially Steps Four to Nine, lead us into an experience of forgiveness, healing and, we hope, reconciliation, a path to new life, a lush garden free from weeds.

Healing as an Exodus Journey and Paschal Mystery Experience

Louis O.	Drunk	Sober	12 Steps	Dry Drunk	Recovery	Happy, Free Sobriety
Moses	Slavery Egypt	Red Sea Freedom	10 Commandments	40 Years in the desert	Crossing the Jordan	The Promised Land
Jesus	Passion	Death	Resurrection	Appearances	Ascension	Pentecost
Us	Hurt	Loss	Survival	Grieving	Forgiveness	New Life

Illustration 25

Have you ever heard comments such as "forget the past" or "let sleeping dogs lie"?

Experience has taught me that dealing with the past through the Twelve Step program is much more positive and life-giving.

In 1977, Louis O. visited me after an A.A. Roundup and shared some of his story. An alcoholic for 12 years, he found Alcoholics Anonymous and sobered up. For the next four years, taken up with this new program, he travelled the north, trying to spread the message of A.A. Then, suddenly, he ended up in hospital with a heart condition. This gave him an opportunity to reflect on his life and his newfound sobriety. It dawned on him that though he was sober, not much else had changed in his life. He was still tense, worried, empty and often miserable. His family did not feel any better off – at times they wished he were back drinking. He realized that he had been on a dry drunk for four years, and was not really working the program.

That realization brought a new resolve to really work the Twelve Steps. With a deeper understanding of his own powerlessness, his faith in God's power to heal him grew stronger (Steps One and Two).

He made a decision to surrender his life and will to that Higher Power (Step Three). Then Louis signed himself out of the hospital, threw away the medication and continued this new way of life with a searching and fearless moral inventory of his whole life (Step Four). Next he shared this painful truth with God and another human being (Step Five).

He then went on to deal with his anger and resentment by learning to forgive those who hurt him, and dealt with the losses in his life through acceptance (Steps Six and Seven). He made amends as best he could to the people he had hurt (Steps Eight and Nine), and finally began to experience peace and freedom to share his growth with others (Steps Ten to Twelve). As he ended his story, he asked if we could pray together, which we did. Then he left.

After the door closed behind him, I sat there for some time in silent wonder, amazed at the transformation in this man. I marvelled at how it had happened through the Twelve Step program. But there was more to it than that. Another faint, tantalizing thought was teasing my mind and continued to haunt me for days until it dawned on me. Louis's story was familiar, because I had heard it before.

The Exodus journey! Louis had experienced the same transforming reality in his life as the Hebrew people in the desert. Their story was one of centuries of slavery that came to an end only after the plagues and the death of the Egyptian firstborn convinced Pharaoh to let the people go. They then experienced political liberation as they crossed the Red Sea. Next came Mt. Sinai and the Ten Commandments, followed by 40 years wandering in the desert, where they learned two important things: to trust God one day at a time (manna in the morning for that day only; quail every evening) and to look upon a bronze serpent raised on a standard when they were bitten, a serpent that had no poison in it.

This incident is found in Numbers 21:8-9: "And the Lord said to Moses, 'Make a poisonous serpent and set it on a pole; and everyone who is bitten shall look at it and live.' So Moses made a serpent of bronze, and put it upon a pole; and whenever a serpent bit someone, that person would look at the serpent of bronze and live." This serpent on a standard is a symbol of the Higher Power in whom there is no addiction. Those who profess the Christian faith would naturally see this standard as a prophetic prefiguring of Jesus, the sinless one, hanging on the cross. Jesus himself states this truth clearly in John 3:14-15, "And just as Moses lifted up the serpent in the wilderness, so must the Son of Man be lifted up, that whoever believes in him may have eternal life." Finally, after learning these key lessons and teachings, the Hebrew people crossed over the Jordan River and entered the Promised Land.

The similarity between the two stories is striking. For the Hebrew people, there were six stages of *deliverance*: slavery in Egypt, liberation through the Red Sea, Mt. Sinai and the Ten Commandments, a 40-year desert experience, crossing the Jordan, and entering the Promised Land.

For Louis, there were six stages of *recovery*: addiction, sobriety, the Twelve Step program, four years as a dry drunk, recovery, and finally, happy, free sobriety. He had been through an Exodus journey.

As I reflected on this new awareness, I intuited that there was more. The Paschal Mystery! This familiar story reveals the same pattern as the previous two stories. Louis had experienced the Paschal Mystery, a life-transforming event that was foreshadowed by the Exodus journey and the passion, death and resurrection of Jesus.

For Jesus, the Paschal Lamb, there were six stages of *transformation*: passion (his abuse by the soldiers and religious leaders and especially his moral loneliness), death on the Cross, resurrection, appearances to his disciples, ascension into heaven, and Pentecost (the sending of the Spirit on his followers). It was the same pattern for Louis. He had experienced the Paschal Mystery through the Twelve Steps.

Louis' years of active addiction were his *passion*. His *death* was his newfound sobriety. Finding the Twelve Step program was his *resurrection*, enabling him to survive. Working the steps, dealing with his hurt and grieving his losses were the *appearances* of Jesus for him. Forgiving the hurt, letting go of the anger and accepting the losses in his life were his *ascension*. Finally, experiencing a new life of happy, free sobriety and genuine recovery were his *Pentecost*.

It can be the same for us. We can enter into the same six stages of healing life's hurts and having our lives transformed into greater peace, joy and freedom by living our faith and working the Twelve Steps.

Our passion is our life's *hurts*, leaving us angry, resentful and bitter. Our death is the *losses* in our lives, leaving us sad, full of self-pity and often stuck in grief. Our resurrection is our coping skills that enabled us to *survive*. The problem is that surviving life is not enough. Too many people settle for survival, which is similar to remaining a victim. We are meant to thrive: to live life to the full, not merely to survive it. Those in A.A. put it this way: "We have survived life; now we must learn to live it."

The *appearances* become for us a time of healing and grieving. This stage helps us move beyond mere survival. Jesus appeared to Mary Magdalene in the garden after his resurrection and later to his disciples to teach them to grieve and to mourn his loss. He was the same Jesus, but he had changed. Now he was the Risen Lord. However, he could not send them his Spirit unless they let go of him physically. That was why he told Mary Magdalene not to cling to him, for he had not yet ascended to the Father. She was to have faith that, although she would no longer be able to see him, he would be more present to her through the gift of his Spirit than he was before (John 20:17).

Jesus wants to teach us this same lesson. We also have to deal with our hurt by expressing our anger in a positive, loving manner, and to face our losses by grieving and mourning them. We reach the stage where we are finally able to forgive the hurt by letting go of the anger and resentment, and to accept the losses by letting go of the sadness and self-pity. In so doing, we create a space into which God can pour the Spirit of forgiveness for the hurt and acceptance of whatever loss we have experienced. Through this *forgiveness and acceptance*, our Ascension happens.

In the case of loss of loved ones, when we have adequately mourned their loss, have truly let them go and have given them back to God, we can receive their spirit to be with us in a new way. We are then ready to experience Pentecost as a *new life* of peace, joy and freedom, including the sense of the presence of our loved ones with us spiritually. We will have had our own Exodus journey and Paschal Mystery experience of deep inner healing, as did Louis.

So forgetting the past and letting sleeping dogs lie are not the real answers. Dealing with our hurt and loss through an active faith is. And the Twelve Step program, available to all, is a ready guide to anyone wanting to really live life to the full, rather than just survive it.

Stepping Through the Exodus Journey and Paschal Mystery Experience

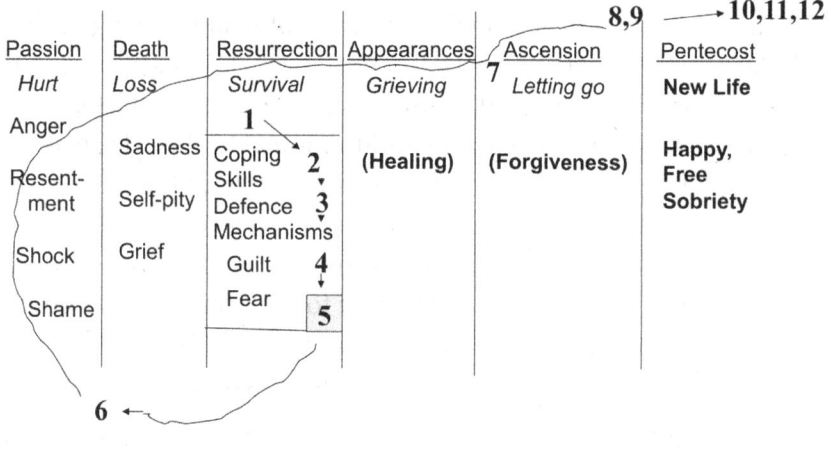

Illustration 26

This biblical model of the Twelve Step program has taken us to the heart of its dynamic power to heal. Anyone who works the program diligently and prayerfully will actually experience the same process of liberation that the Hebrew people experienced thousands of years ago in the crossing of the Red Sea and in the journey through the Sinai desert. Even more important, they will experience the same Paschal Mystery that Jesus shared with his disciples and wants to share with us.

Looking at *Illustration 26*, we see that the journey begins with Step One, placed precisely where so many people are situated, in survival mode within an invisible spiritual cage. One might be sober, but for many of us, our lives still border on the chaotic. We need to move on to deeper healing.

Step Two takes us clockwise and downward a little deeper into that spiritual cage, where we come to believe that a power greater than ourselves can restore us to sanity, heal us and transform us. In this stage, we are like a caterpillar in a chrysalis, waiting to be transformed into a beautiful butterfly.

Step Three continues that clockwise downward thrust, deeper into our painful reality, as we make a decision to surrender our stubborn self-will and our lives into the hands of this Higher Power as we understand that Higher Power.

Step Four then asks us to look at the ways we acted out of our pain instead of forgiving. We see how we hurt our God, other people and ourselves, and how we fell out of touch with and wounded God's creation.

Step Five takes us out of our invisible spiritual cage as we step through the door of humility by sharing the darkest part of our past with God, ourselves and another human being. We are truly starting to heal and to experience liberation from the guilt and fear that we may have carried for years.

Now with Step Six, we continue to circle clockwise and backward, to address the anger and resentment, shame and sadness, self-pity and grief we carry in our lives. We name and claim all this mess as our own, and open ourselves up to receiving the healing power of God as God removes these defects of character one by one through our Step Seven prayer and the power of the Holy Spirit.

Step Six takes us on a quantum leap forward towards forgiveness and healing. We let go of anger and resentment through the spiritual gift of forgiveness. We let go of sadness and self-pity through the spiritual gift of acceptance. We begin to experience inner serenity and well-being. We are almost ready to emerge as butterflies.

Steps Eight and Nine lead us to experience more forgiveness from the people we hurt as we make amends to them all, continuing our healing journey towards reconciliation and healing.

Steps Ten to Twelve now take us into the Promised Land, not to rest on our laurels, but to continue to heal and grow with a new serenity, freedom, joy and happiness that transcends any that we had known before. We are beginning to experience the reign of God vibrating within us and among us. It doesn't get any better than this. We are flying into the future like new butterflies. The Twelve Steps have become for us both an Old Testament Exodus journey and a New Testament Paschal Mystery experience.

The Spiritual Spiral

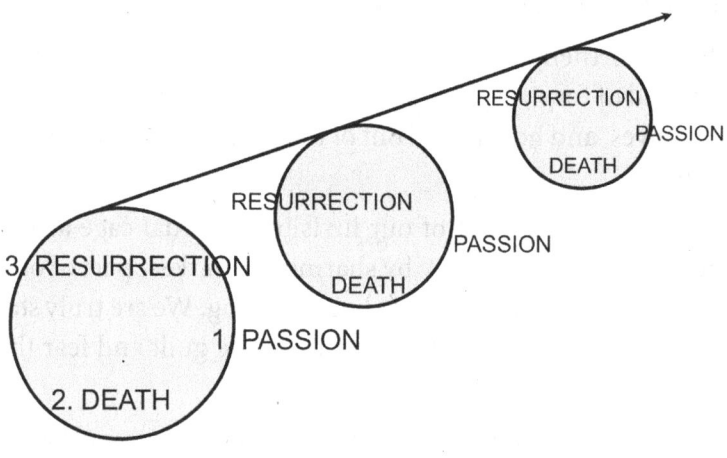

Illustration 27

For many people, the image of the spiritual journey is like that of climbing a ladder into heaven, which requires a certain amount of effort and involves slipping off a rung at times, along with our fear of falling.

This was the image I had as I was growing up. In 1976, a retreat master shattered that image once and for all simply by drawing a spiral on the board. He explained that this was how we grew personally and spiritually, following a spiral path downward to a bottom, then around and up to a new level, rather than climbing a ladder. This theory aligns with the three stages for spiritual growth used by the spiritual masters like St. John of the Cross: *purgation, illumination* and *union*. It is also the process that the Twelve Steps lead us into.

When we become aware of some wrongdoing, some defect of character in our life, this painful truth is our passion, leading us downward on the spiral into a painful descent to an experience that is like a death. This is the stage of *purgation* or purification.

As we admit this defect or sin, and address it with humble honesty through faith, self-awareness and fellowship, we let God in to remove that sin or defect of character and begin to move upward. This is the stage of *illumination*.

The process leads us into an experience of growth as forgiveness and healing that is our resurrection. We rise, not to where we were before, but to a new level of living life more fully, with greater joy. This is the stage of *union*.

The simple secret to this Paschal Mystery is that the circles grow smaller, indicating less stress and pain each time we deal with an issue in our lives, and the line between the circles is always moving upward, indicating healing and growth.

Living this spiritual spiral, we enter into a new world of loving, sharing, sacrificing, forgiving and serenity. According to the spiritual writer Demetrius Dumm, O.S.B.,

> This peace is not just the absence of war or dissension. It has profound positive implications suggesting a state of supreme wellbeing, the sense of being fully accepted, of being in exactly the right place at exactly the right time. There is a profound contentment but not smugness. This kind of peace can be given only by God since it reflects the deep sense of freedom and confidence that comes from knowing and feeling the love of God.[56]

The Big Book adds the assurance that "life will take on new meaning. To watch people recover, to see them help others, to watch loneliness vanish, to see a fellowship grow up about you, to have a host of friends – this is an experience you must not miss."[57]

Life ignites as we enter into an adventure with the Spirit. We have a new sense of who we are and who we are becoming, the persons we are meant to be, images of God, who is love. Such is the power of the Twelve Step program. It works if we work it!

Suggested Activities

1. Recall a specific time in your life when you experienced real healing.
2. Try to identify which of the recovery experiences/models described in this chapter best describes the process that your specific healing involved.
3. Spend some time in prayer, expressing gratitude to our God and loving Higher Power for the healing that has happened in your life.
4. If no specific healing emerges for you, what need for healing might the contents of this chapter be pointing out to you? Take some concrete steps to move towards that healing in your life.

A Case Study: Part Two

"Achieving Intimacy with My Father"

As mentioned in the Case Study: Part One at the outset of this book, this part will provide completion to the story presented there. By way of review, as a teenager, as a young adult and even as a young priest, I had struggled in my relationship with my father. It took me 15 years to learn to forgive him for his shortcomings and to let go of the anger I self-righteously harboured towards him. Of course, I thought I was right all along. Finally, in an almost miraculous way, through the Twelve Step program, I was able to come to my senses, deal with my anger, forgive my father and be reconciled with him two years before he died. I am grateful for this experience that helped me to truly celebrate his funeral.

Eleven years later, I was urged by my spiritual director at an Oblate renewal program in San Antonio, Texas, to avail myself of the services of a counsellor. I resisted initially, thinking that I had done enough counselling and therapy to that point. My spiritual director, the late Andy Wueste, O.M.I., persisted, God bless him. I finally relented and found a counsellor in the Yellow Pages.

After at least two sessions of rather half-heartedly repeating my story, including my struggle with my father, the counsellor suddenly stopped me. He told me that "acting out of anger towards my father was not the same as sitting down with my father and sharing my feelings of anger with him."

Shocked, I realized that I had never done that. Sure, we had forgiven each other, had been reconciled and had two good years together before he died, during which time we could talk about many things, like politics, farming, relatives, religion, etc., without that old, familiar tension between us. However, we had never talked about "us," about our relationship. I had never shared with him those strong emotions that I had felt for years towards him.

I instinctively knew that I had to do Steps Six and Seven regarding my relationship with my father at a deeper level than ever before. I entered into a *poustinia*, a one-day retreat at the Oblate retreat house in San Antonio, and wrote a seven-page letter to my father, sharing all the feelings that I had never shared with him while he was alive. Then I read the letter out loud to a pillow on a chair representing my father, and shed a few tears.

A week later, at our next session, the counsellor asked me what that experience was like. Noticing my struggle to answer his question, he asked if he could help me. When I nodded in affirmation, he asked me if it was more like an "adult to adult" relationship now with my father. I resonated strongly with that question. That was it, exactly! I had grown up. I was no longer the "little boy" and he the "big daddy." By means of that humble, honest letter to my father that shared my emotions about "us" and about our relationship, he and I were now friends. I had shared my feelings with him, as well as having become aware of what his feelings were.

For the first time in my life, 11 years after my father died, I had achieved intimacy with him. On the way home, the colour of the world was somehow brighter. It was as if I had put on amber motorcycle goggles. Then there dawned on me a powerful awareness of the Communion of Saints: if I was healing in my relationship with my father here on earth because of that humble letter, then I believe he was healing in his relationship with me.

Ron Rolheiser speaks of one definition of purgatory as "the pain of entering heaven." I had a profound sense that I was actually helping my father enter heaven. It doesn't get better than that. It was then that I believe I received the spirit of my father to be present to me in a new way, the way that Jesus promised to be present to us after his ascension through the gift of his Spirit at Pentecost.

This may be unfamiliar language to those who are not of the Catholic faith, but for me, this insight, awareness and experience were a particularly beautiful and healing gift that served as a crescendo to my whole healing journey, one for which I am eternally grateful to our Creator God and loving Higher Power. I hope and pray that you, the reader, will also experience that same spiritual power at work in unique and wonderful ways suited to you and your life through the Twelve Step program, to establish you solidly within a life of sobriety that is joyous and free.

Conclusion

We have completed a Twelve Step journey of faith that I hope has helped you deepen your own healing venture. Beginning with our own wonderful but wounded humanity, we have explored the world of spirituality as well as the reality of addiction and recovery from addiction through the Twelve Step program.

The goal of this book was to provide insights, stories, experiences, ideas and principles all connected with the Twelve Steps, which, if practised, will move the reader towards a greater degree of personal freedom and happy sobriety.

The continual emergence of new addictions, such as texting, pornography and even "being right," underlines the need for this kind of book. I hope that these pages can be of some help to those struggling with any addiction in their lives and/or those trying to journey with and understand someone in their family or circle of friends who is addicted.

I want to close with the refrain that has resounded throughout the years at the end of many support group meetings: "Keep coming back – it works, if you work it!" May we all be blessed with constant growth into a new path of sobriety and life that is joyous and free.

Bibliography and Suggested Reading

Alcoholics Anonymous. New York: Alcoholics Anonymous World Services, 1976.

Bass, Ellen, and Laura Davis. *The Courage to Heal.* 3rd ed. New York: Harper Perennial, 1994.

Beattie, Melody. *Beyond Codependency and Getting Better All the Time.* Center City, MN: Hazeldon Foundation, 1989.

Booth, Fr. Leo. *When God Becomes a Drug.* New York: Jeremy P. Tarcher, 1976.

Bradshaw, John. *Bradshaw On: The Family: A New Way of Creating Solid Self-Esteem.* Deerfield Beach, FL: Health Communications, Inc., 1988.

Carroll, John E. *Contemplation in Action.* New York: Crossroad, 2006.

Chittister, Joan. *The Fire in These Ashes: A Spirituality of Contemporary Religious Life.* Kansas City: Sheed & Ward, 1995.

———. *In Search of Belief.* Missouri: Ligouri/Triumph, 1999.

Corretto, Carlo. *Letters from the Desert.* London: Darton, Longman & Todd, 1972.

Donovan, Vincent. *Christianity Rediscovered.* Maryknoll, NY: Orbis Books, 1982.

Dorf, Francis. *The Art of Passing Over.* New York: Paulist Press, 1988.

Dumm, Demetrius. *Flowers in the Desert: A Spirituality of the Bible.* New York: Paulist Press, 1987.

Finley, James. *Merton's Palace of Nowhere.* rev. ed. Notre Dame, IN: Ave Maria Press, 2003.

Frank, Anne. *The Diary of a Young Girl.* New York: Doubleday, 1967.

Glasser, Dr. William. *Reality Therapy.* New York: Harper & Row, 1965.

Gorski, Terence T. *Passages through Recovery.* Center City, MN: Hazelden, 1989.

Hemfelt, Dr. Robert and Dr. Richard Fowler. *Serenity: A Companion for Twelve Step Recovery.* Nashville: Thomas Nelson, 1990.

Jacobs, Durand F. *Compulsive Gambling: Theory, Research, and Practice.* Lexington, MA: Lexington Books, 1989.

James, William. *Variety of Religious Experience.* New York: Modern Library, 1936.

John of the Cross. "Maxims and Counsels," in *The Collected Works of St. John of the Cross,* Kieran Kavanaugh, O.C.D. and Otilio Rodriquez, O.C.D., trans. Washington, D.C.: ICS Publications, 1979.

Keating, Thomas. *Divine Therapy and Addiction.* New York: Lantern Books, 2009.

Kennedy, Eugene. *The Pain of Being Human.* Chicago: Thomas More Press, 1972.

Kidd, Sue Monk. *The Secret Life of Bees.* Penguin Books, 2002.

Kübler-Ross, Dr. Elisabeth. *On Death and Dying.* New York: Scribner, 1969.

Kurtz, Ernest, and Katherine Ketchum. *A Spirituality of Imperfection.* New York: Bantam Books, 1994.

Kushner, Harold S. *When Bad Things Happen to Good People.* New York: Schocken Books, 1981.

Lavoie, Sylvain. *Together We Heal.* Toronto: Novalis, 2014.

Mackey, Larry. *Bountyfull Healing.* Ottawa: Novalis, 2005.

Martin, James, S.J. *My Life with the Saints.* Chicago: Loyola Press, 2006.

Masini, Mario. *Lectio Divina.* New York: Society of St. Paul, 1998.

Maslow, Abraham. *Motivation and Human Personality.* New York: Harper & Row, 1954.

May, Gerald. *Addiction and Grace.* San Francisco: Harper & Row, 1988.

———. *Will and Spirit.* San Francisco: HarperSanFrancisco, 1982.

Meier, Augustine, and Peter VanKatwyk, eds. *The Challenge of Forgiveness.* Ottawa: Novalis, 2001.

Merton, Thomas. *Thoughts in Solitude: Reflections on the Spiritual Life and the Love of Solitude.* Garden City, NY: Image Books 1968.

McGoey, John H. *Through Sex to Love.* Toronto: Gall Publications, 1976.

Monbourquette, John. *How to Forgive.* Ottawa: Novalis, 2000.

———. *How to Befriend Your Shadow.* Ottawa: Novalis, 2001.

Nakken, Craig. *The Addictive Personality.* New York: Harper & Row, 1988.

Napan, Ksenijaa, "Being, Loving and Contributing," in *Spirituality and Social Care: Contributing to Personal and Community Well-being.* Mary Nash and Bruce Stewart, eds. Philadelphia: Jessica Kingsley Publishers, 2002.

Nemeck, Francis Kelly, and Marie Theresa Coombs. *The Spiritual Journey: Critical Thresholds and Stages of Adult Spiritual Genesis.* Wilmington, DE: Michael Glazier, 1988.

———. *O Blessed Night! Recovering from Addiction, Codependency, and Attachment Based on the Insights of St. John of the Cross and Pierre Teilhard de Chardin.* New York: The Society of St. Paul, 1991.

Niebuhr, Reinhold. *The Irony of American History.* New York: Scribners, 1952.

O'Leary, Daniel. *Already Within.* Dublin: Columba Press in association with *The Tablet*, 2007.

One Day at a Time in Al-anon. Virginia Beach, VA: Al-anon Family Group Headquarters.

Peck, Scott. *The Road Less Traveled.* New York: Simon and Schuster, 1979.

Philibert, Paul. *The Priesthood of the Faithful: Key to a Living Church.* Collegeville, MN: Liturgical Press, 2005.

Rogers, Carl. *On Becoming a Person.* Boston: Houghton Mifflin, 1961.

Rohr, Richard. *Adam's Return.* New York: Crossroads, 2004.

———. *Breathing Under Water.* Cincinnati, OH: St. Anthony Messenger Press, 2011.

———. *Falling Upward: A Spirituality for the Two Halves of Life.* San Francisco: Jossey-Bass, 2011.

———. *From Wild Man to Wise Man.* Cincinnati, OH: St. Anthony Messenger Press, 2005.

———. *Hope Against Darkness.* Cincinnati, OH: St. Anthony Messenger Press, 2001.

———. *Immortal Diamond.* San Francisco: Jossey-Bass, 2013.

Rolheiser, Ronald. *Holy Longing: The Search for a Christian Spirituality.* New York: Doubleday, 1999.

———. *Sacred Fire.* New York: Image Books, 2014.

———. "Spirituality an Erotic Urge," www.ronrolheiser.com, December 6, 1982.

———. *The Shattered Lantern*. London: Hodder & Stoughton, 1995.

Rovers, Martin, "Forgiveness and Post-Affair Marital Counselling: A Systemic Perspective," in *The Challenge of Forgiveness*. Augustine Meier and Peter Van Katwyk, eds. Ottawa: Novalis, 2001.

Sanford, John. *The Man Who Wrestled with God*. New York: Paulist Press, 1987.

Smedes, Lewis B. *Forgive and Forget*. New York: HarperCollins, 1996.

Twelve Steps and Twelve Traditions. New York: Al-Anon Family Group Headquarters, Inc., 1987.

Tyrell, Bernard J. *Christotherapy*. New York: Seabury Press, 1975.

Vanier, Jean. *Becoming Human*. New York: Paulist Press, 1998.

———. *Eruption to Hope*. Toronto: Griffin House, 1971.

List of Illustrations

PART ONE: HUMAN BE-ING

01: The Medicine Wheel 21
02: The Lake of Our Humanity 22
03: The Awareness Wheel 40
04: The Wellness Wheel of Met Needs 42

PART TWO: A SPIRITUALITY OF RECOVERY AND WELLNESS

05: Teepee Spirituality 48
06: Fellowship = Love and Intimacy 53
07: Teepee Spirituality, Human Needs
     and the Great Commandment 57
08: A Spirituality of Human Incompleteness 59

PART THREE: THE JOURNEY INTO ADDICTION

09: The Dysfunctional Wheel 69
10: The Journey into Addiction 80
11: The Spiritual Cage 96
12: Our Spiritual Burden 98

PART FOUR: THE TWELVE STEP HEALING JOURNEY

13: The Twelve Step Healing Journey 104
14: Powerlessness: Foundation for a New Life 108
15: The God of Our Understanding 118
16: A Compassionate Higher Power 120
17: Moral Inventory 125
18: Prayer: A Muskeg Image of life 166

PART FIVE: UNDERSTANDING AND INTEGRATING THE TWELVE STEPS

19: The Recovery Wheel 179
20: The Twelve Steps Applied to Teepee Spirituality 182
21: The Recovery Burger 185
22: Our Spiritual Burden and the Twelve Steps 186
23: The Healing Hamburger 188
24: A Spirituality of Weeding 190
25: Healing as an Exodus Journey and Paschal Mystery Experience 192
26: Stepping Through the Exodus Journey and Paschal Mystery Experience 196
27: The Spiritual Spiral 198

Appendix 1

THE TWELVE STEPS OF ALCOHOLICS ANONYMOUS

1. We admitted we were powerless over alcohol – that our lives had become unmanageable.
2. Came to believe that a Power greater than ourselves could restore us to sanity.
3. Made a decision to turn our will and our lives over to the care of God *as we understood Him.*
4. Made a searching and fearless moral inventory of ourselves.
5. Admitted to God, to ourselves, and to another human being the exact nature of our wrongs.
6. Were entirely ready to have God remove all these defects of character.
7. Humbly asked Him to remove our shortcomings.
8. Made a list of all persons we had harmed, and became willing to make amends to them all.
9. Made direct amends to such people wherever possible, except when to do so would injure them or others.
10. Continued to take personal inventory and when we were wrong promptly admitted it.
11. Sought through prayer and meditation to improve our conscious contact with God *as we understood Him,* praying only for knowledge of His will for us and the power to carry that out.
12. Having had a spiritual awakening as the result of these steps, we tried to carry this message to alcoholics, and to practice these principles in all our affairs.[58]

Disclaimer

The Twelve Steps are reprinted and adapted with permission of Alcoholics Anonymous World Services, Inc. (A.A.W.S.). Permission to reprint and adapt the Twelve Steps does not mean that A.A.W.S. has reviewed or approved the contents of this publication, or that A.A.W.S. necessarily agrees with the views expressed herein. A.A. is a program of recovery from alcoholism <u>only</u> – use of the Twelve Steps in connection with programs and activities which are patterned after A.A., but which address other problems, or in any other non-A.A. context, does not imply otherwise.

(General Service Office, New York, June 2013)

Appendix 2

CONCERNED INTERVENTION

Early in my experience of the Twelve Step program, I happened to see a movie on concerned intervention that has proved helpful in my ministry over the years. In the past, a hard, confrontational approach was often used. More recently, professionals in this field would advise a gentler approach of conversations expressing concern, then warnings and a measured increase of requests for changes in behaviour.

If nothing changes, then those who care about the addict and have some influence over him or her gather to plan an intervention designed to get that person into treatment. Each one records specific incidents they have observed, including the time and place of addictive behaviour. It is wise to obtain the services of a competent facilitator to coordinate the material and plan the intervention to maximize its effectiveness. The group then meets with the addict at an opportune time to present the person with their material, express their concern for him or her, and present options for treatment and definite consequences of a refusal.

My first intervention involved a maintenance man at the local hospital who was abusing alcohol. After some expressions of concern, the administrator and I met with him to give him one more opportunity to change. If there were any further incidents, he would have a choice – retire or go for treatment. We made the necessary phone calls to line up both possibilities, including his replacement at work, depending on his choice.

Sure enough, a few weeks after the intervention, he dented the fender of his beloved vehicle while he was under the influence of alcohol. We met with him as we had promised, and gave him the two options – retire or go for treatment. He begged for another chance.

We stood firm and gave him the choice between the two options. He again begged for another chance. I remember well reaching for the phone, telling him that both places were ready to receive him and asking which one should I dial – the retirement home or the treatment facility?

Realizing that we were serious, and not wanting at all to retire, he chose treatment. I placed the call immediately, in his presence, to say that he was on his way. He left the next morning, since the transportation had all been arranged. He underwent two and a half months of treatment, and did well. He managed three years of happy, free sobriety, with only one relapse, before he died of a heart attack.

Years later, I was involved in another intervention in which we did not closely follow the principles outlined above; instead, we used a very tough approach. The results were a lot of unnecessary pain, confusion and a dubious outcome fraught with bruised feelings and unresolved issues that only time, it seems, might heal. I learned the hard way that a carefully planned, compassionate, yet firm and well-executed intervention is worth the cost and time it takes to do it well.

Appendix 3

THE SACRAMENT OF RECONCILIATION AND THE TWELVE STEPS

As I delved more and more into the healing power of the Twelve Step program, used it for my own recovery and healing, and continued to minister within my faith tradition as a Catholic priest and later as an archbishop, it dawned on me that there was a very interesting correlation of the Twelve Steps of Alcoholics Anonymous with the whole process of sacramental reconciliation within the Catholic Church. This correlation also revealed a weakness in the practice of the Catholic faith; the absence of a focus on healing that the Twelve Step program can help restore to the Church.

Since the renewal of the Second Vatican Council, we have deepened our understanding of what we used to call "confession." We see it more in the light of the relationship of the whole person with the community as well as with God. We have come to see that sin is never really private or an individual affair, but affects the whole community, the Body of Christ. We also see restoring wholeness to the person not as an individual act but as a whole process that should ritually involve the community. This new understanding is reflected in the terms we now use instead of simply "going to confession." We use terms like "Penance," or even better, "Sacrament of Reconciliation," because this more accurately describes the inner depths of this sacrament.

Traditionally for the Church, the stages of reconciliation are (1) sorrow, contrition and a desire to change, (2) an examination of conscience, (3) confession to a priest and absolution, (4) the imposition of a penance, and (5) reconciliation and new life.

Placing the stages of reconciliation side by side with the Twelve Steps yields the following graph:

Sacrament	Twelve Step Program
1. Sorrow, contrition and a desire to change	Steps 1–3 (Powerlessness: I can't; He can; I'll let Him.)
2. Examination of conscience	Step 4 (Searching and fearless moral inventory)
3. Confession and absolution	Step 5 (Admit to God, to self and to one other person the exact nature of my wrongs)
4. *(Healing of sinfulness)*	Steps 6 & 7 (Ask God to remove these defects of character)
5. Penance	Steps 8 & 9 (Listed those harmed and made amends to them all)
6. Reconciliation	Steps 10–12 (Daily inventory, prayer, sharing and a new life of happy, free sobriety)

As you can see, there are six stages now, not only five, due to the focus on Steps Six and Seven. What was missing in the Church is the fourth stage, shown above in italics – an emphasis on healing. The weakness in the way the Church has been practising this sacrament over the centuries reveals itself in Steps Six and Seven, with their focus on healing. For many cradle Catholics, confession was rather repetitious, a clearing of the slate, a penance of prayer rather than making amends, and an unfortunate mentality of filling the slate up again until the next confession.

One older man who was confronted with love by the young girl he had abused showed no remorse. He gave a lame excuse when she asked for an apology. That attitude left both the young girl and me angry and disappointed. When I pleaded with him a few days later to do more than this, to give her a genuine apology, he responded that he had taken care of it in confession. Such was, and perhaps still is, the attitude and thinking of many to this day.

Thankfully, healing is at the core and heart of the Twelve Step program. Mind you, even for many in the program, these steps are not well understood or worked. What surfaced for me was an awareness that could be of mutual benefit to both the Church and those in the program. The healing dimension that is at the heart of both recovery modes needs more emphasis, an emphasis that I have since tried to underline in all my presentations and to practise in all my celebrations of reconciliation.

Appendix 4

TWELVE BY TWENTY-FOUR

Starting the day: Steps 1, 2, 3, 6, 7, 11

Start each day with a sincere, simple prayer from the heart (prayer of the *Anawim*, the poor who know they need God) that establishes conscious contact with God and includes within it the steps listed above. For example:

Creator God and loving parent, good morning and thank you for this day, this gift of 24 hours, which you give to me out of love. (Step 11)

Lord, I come before you aware of my brokenness, powerlessness, weakness and sinfulness. I can't live this day the way you want me to, joyous and free, without your help, so I surrender this day to you. (Steps 1 and 3)

Please fill me with your Holy Spirit, just for today. Give me a spirit of faith, hope, love, peace, joy, purity, humility, wisdom, patience, forgiveness, etc. … (Name whatever you need, and believe that God can make a difference as you pray.) (Step 2)

Deliver me from my character defects today … false pride, control, insecurity, resentment, self-pity, stubbornness, etc. … (Name the defects you are struggling with.) (Steps 6 and 7)

During the day: Step 12

Try to speak a positive word to anyone who may need encouragement. Be willing to share your experiences, strengths, weaknesses and feelings with anyone who needs a helping hand.

Finishing the day: Steps 4, 5, 6, 7, 8, 9, 10, 11

Look back over the day – your actions, thoughts, attitudes and feelings – humbly and honestly (Step 10). Admit whatever you may have done wrong (Step 4) and share this with God and another person if you can, perhaps with your spouse or a friend (Step 5). If you are aware that you may have hurt someone, try to check it out. If this is so, and if it is possible, ask forgiveness and make amends (by letter or phone, if need be), or at least decide to do so at the earliest opportunity (Steps 8 and 9). Try to forgive anyone who has hurt you this day, praying for the ability to do so (Steps 6 and 7).

End with some of your favourite prayers, perhaps the Our Father or the Serenity Prayer, or give thanks to God in your own words (Step 11).

+ Sylvain Lavoie, OMI
Archbishop emeritus of Keewatin-The Pas

Appendix 5

THE TWELVE STEP BEATITUDES

1. Blessed are the powerless, for theirs is the power of God.
2. Blessed are they who surrender to a Higher Power, for they shall be transformed.
3. Blessed are they who openly admit their wrongs, for they shall receive forgiveness.
4. Blessed are they who are aware of their shortcomings, for they shall be healed.
5. Blessed are they who grieve and mourn, for they shall be consoled.
6. Blessed are they who forgive, let go, and let God, for they shall be at peace.
7. Blessed are they who apologize and make amends, for they shall be reconciled.
8. Blessed are they who walk with God one day at a time, for they will enjoy happy, free sobriety.

+ Sylvain Lavoie, OMI
Archbishop emeritus of Keewatin-The Pas
2014

Other Resources

Healing Soul Pain. An effective program on Trauma Recovery and Grief Support developed by Dr. Jane Simington: www.takingflight international

Returning to Spirit. A program on healing the Indian Residential School legacy, co-developed by Marc Pizandawatc and Sr. Anne Thompson, S.S.A.

Drumming from Within: Stories of Faith and Hope from the Canadian North, by Sylvain Lavoie. Toronto: Novalis, 2010.

Together We Heal: A 12-Step Approach for the Healing of Sex Abuse, by Sylvain Lavoie. Toronto: Novalis, 2009.

Images of Hope: A Spirituality of Recovery Retreat, by Sylvain Lavoie. A set of 8 DVDs, available from the author at the address below for $20 plus shipping.

A PowerPoint presentation of the illustrations in this book is available from the author and will be emailed to those who request it.

AUTHOR'S NOTE

As presentations on this Twelve Step program during retreats and workshops are always in a process of development, new ideas or insights into the program and other feedback from readers on the contents of this book would be greatly appreciated.

Please send your comments to:

Archbishop emeritus Sylvain Lavoie, OMI
20 Gareth Place
St. Albert, AB
Canada, T8N 3K5

sylvainomi@icloud.com
1-587-589-2448 (Cell)
1-780-460-4269 (Residence)
1-780-459-5511 (Office)

Endnotes

1. Joan Chittister, *The Fire in These Ashes: A Spirituality of Contemporary Religious Life* (Kansas City: Sheed & Ward, 1995), 121.
2. John Monbourquette, *How to Forgive* (Ottawa: Novalis, 2000), 116.
3. John Bradshaw, *Bradshaw on the Family* (Deerfield Beach, FL: Health Communications Inc., 1988), 144.
4. James Martin, *My Life with the Saints* (Chicago: Loyola Press, 2006), 387.
5. Ibid.
6. According to Ernest Kurtz and Katherine Ketcham, in footnote 2 of "Introduction: The Story of Spirituality," in *Spirituality of Imperfection* (New York: Bantam Books, 1992), 245, the Rabbi Zusya story, often retold, may be found most conveniently in Martin Buber, *Tales of the Hasidim: The Early Masters* (New York: Schocken Books, 1947), 251.
7. Sue Monk Kidd, *The Secret Life of Bees* (New York: Penguin, 2002), 95.
8. John H. McGoey, *Through Sex to Love* (Toronto: Gall Publications, 1976), 3–4.
9. Gerald May, *Will and Spirit* (New York: Harper Collins, 1982), 71.
10. Ksenijaa Napan, "Being, Loving and Contributing," in *Spirituality and Social Care*, Mary Nash and Bruce Steward, eds. (Philadelphia: Jessica Kingsley Publishers, 2002), 124.
11. Alcoholics Anonymous, *The Big Book* (New York: Alcoholics Anonymous World Services, 1976), 62.
12. May, *Will and Spirit*, 13, 6.
13. Richard Rohr, *Adam's Return* (New York: Crossroads, 2004), 5.
14. James Finley, *Merton's Palace of Nowhere*, rev. ed. (Notre Dame, IN: Ave Maria Press, 2003), 9.
15. Vincent Donovan, *Christianity Rediscovered* (Maryknoll, NY: Orbis Books, 1982), 131ff.
16. Paul Philibert, *The Priesthood of the Faithful* (Collegeville, MN: Liturgical Press, 2005), 109.
17. Ron Rolheiser, *The Holy Longing* (New York: Doubleday, 1999), 3, 4.
18. Anne Frank, *The Diary of a Young Girl* (New York: Doubleday, 1967), entry on February 12, 1944, 134.
19. Daniel O'Leary, *Already Within* (Dublin: Columba Press in association with *The Tablet*, 2007), 123.
20. Ron Rolheiser, "Spirituality an Erotic Urge," found on his website, www.ronrolheiser.com, December 6, 1982. The thoughts that follow on Eros as the basis for our spiritual life are also taken from this article.
21. Richard Rohr, *From Wild Man to Wise Man* (Cincinnati, OH: St. Anthony Messenger Press, 2005), 15. Author's italics.
22. May, *Will and Spirit*, 190.
23. Alcoholics Anonymous, *The Big Book*, 64.
24. Ibid., 122.
25. Ibid., 62.
26. Thomas Keating, *Divine Therapy and Addiction: Centering Prayer and the Twelve Steps* (New York: Lantern Books, 2009), 96. I rearranged the order of the statements that he lists here to coincide more precisely with the three temptations and the order he uses elsewhere.
27. Jean Vanier, *Eruption to Hope* (Toronto: Griffin House, 1971), 26.
28. Ibid., 26.
29. Bradshaw, *Bradshaw on the Family*, 6, 95.
30. Ernest Kurtz and Katherine Ketcham, "Not Magic, but Miracle," in *Spirituality of Imperfection*

(New York: Bantam Books, 1994), 120. In footnotes 5 and 13, they mention that the phrase "locating divinity in drugs" is borrowed from Dr. Leslie Farber in his book of essays entitled *Lying, Despair, Jealousy, Envy, Sex, Suicide, Drugs and the Good Life* (New York: Basic Books, 1976). This phrase appears on page 119.

31 Craig Nakken, *The Addictive Personality* (New York: Harper and Row, 1988), especially 8–10; the World Health Organization quoted by Bradshaw, *Bradshaw on the Family*, 89; and Durand F. "Dewey" Jacobs, *A New Paradigm for Understanding and Treating Addictive Behaviors*, Assembly Room, A. K. Smiley Public Library, November, 1997.

32 Alcoholics Anonymous, *The Big Book*, 58.

33 Monbourquette, *How to Forgive*, 21.

34 Alcoholics Anonymous, *The Big Book*, 58.

35 Terrence Gorski, *Passages Through Recovery* (New York: Hazeldon, 1989), 133.

36 May, *Will and Spirit*, 307.

37 Alcoholics Anonymous, *The Big Book*, 63.

38 Ibid., 58.

39 Carl Jung, quoted in Monbourquette, *How to Forgive*, 163.

40 Müller-Fahrenholz (1997), quoted by Daryold Corbiere Winkler, "Forgiveness and Reconciliation – Lessons from Canada's First Nations," in *The Challenge of Forgiveness*, Augustine Meier and Peter VanKatwyk, eds. (Ottawa: Novalis, 2001), 33.

41 Daniel O'Leary, *Already Within*, 132.

42 Alcoholics Anonymous, *The Big Book*, 76.

43 Reinhold Niebuhr, *The Irony of American History* (New York: Scribners, 1952), 63.

44 Worthington & Drinkard (2000), quoted by Martin Rovers in "Forgiveness in Post-Affair Couple Therapy," in *The Challenge of Forgiveness*, Augustine Meier and Peter Van Katwyk, eds. (Ottawa: Novalis, 2001), 241.

45 Martin, *My Life with the Saints*, 87–88.

46 Thomas Merton, *Thoughts in Solitude* (New York: Image Books, 1968), 81.

47 Donovan, *Christianity Rediscovered*, 131ff.

48 Keating, *Divine Therapy and Addiction*, 151–52. Here he is echoing John of the Cross, who speaks of God speaking in eternal silence (*# 21)*, and hearing in silent love (*# 53)*, "Maxims and Counsels," in *The Collected Works of St. John of the Cross*, Kieran Kavanaugh, O.C.D. and Otilio Rodriquez, O.C.D. trans. (Washington, DC: ICS Publications, 1979).

49 May, *Will and Spirit*, 337 (n. 42).

50 Mario Masini, *Lectio Divina* (New York: Society of St. Paul, 1998), 57.

51 May, *Will and Spirit*, 314, 316, 317.

52 Sr. Joan L. Roccasalvo, C.S.J., Catholic News Agency (December 5, 2012).

53 Bill W., *The Next Frontier: Emotional Sobriety*, January 1958, quoted by Keating in Appendix A of *Divine Therapy and Addiction*, 212.

54 Alcoholics Anonymous, *The Big Book*, 124.

55 Ibid., 153.

56 Demetrius Dumm, OSB, *Flowers in the Desert: A Spirituality of the Bible* (New York: Paulist Press, 1987), 160.

57 Alcoholics Anonymous, *The Big Book*, 89.

58 Ibid., 59.

MARQUIS

Québec, Canada

Printed on Rolland Enviro.
This paper contains 100% post-consumer fiber,
is manufactured using renewable energy - Biogas
and processed chlorine free.

 PCF